Henry VI – Part I

A Play By
William Shakespeare

Henry VI – Part I
by William Shakespeare

ISBN: 978-93-94973-30-5

Published by

DOUBLE 9 BOOKS

2/13-B, Ansari Road
Daryaganj, New Delhi - 110002
info@double9books.com
www.double9books.com
Tel. 011-40042856

Printed in India.

About the Author

William Shakespeare was an English artist and dramatist, broadly viewed as the best essayist in the English language and one of the world's pre-famous playwrights. His magnetic works comprise 38 plays, 154 pieces, two long story sonnets, and a few other sonnets.

Shakespeare was brought up in Stratford-upon-Avon. He was 18 when he got married to Anne Hathaway, with whom he had three kids: Susanna, and twins Hamnet and Judith. Somewhere in the period between 1585 and 1592, he started to professionally work in London as an entertainer, author, and part proprietor of the playing organization then called 'the Lord Chamberlain's Men', later known as the King's Men'. Very few records on Shakespeare's personal life have been collected by now which has led to significant speculations and research on matters such as his sexuality, strict convictions, and whether the works ascribed to him were composed by others.

Shakespeare delivered the greater part of his known work somewhere between 1590 and 1613. He was a highly regarded writer and dramatist in his days. However, his standing didn't ascend to its current statures until the nineteenth century. The Romantics acclaimed Shakespeare as a virtuoso and the legends of the Victorian era adored him. Irish novelist, Bernard Shaw termed the word 'bardolatry' in his honor. In the 20th century, his work was rediscovered by new developments in grant and execution.

Contents

ACT V

ACT I

SCENE I. Westminster Abbey.

Dead March. Enter the Funeral of KING HENRY the Fifth, attended on by Dukes of BEDFORD, Regent of France; GLOUCESTER, Protector; and EXETER, Earl of WARWICK, the BISHOP OF WINCHESTER, Heralds, & c

BEDFORD

Hung be the heavens with black, yield day to night!
Comets, importing change of times and states,
Brandish your crystal tresses in the sky,
And with them scourge the bad revolting stars
That have consented unto Henry's death!
King Henry the Fifth, too famous to live long!
England ne'er lost a king of so much worth.

GLOUCESTER

England ne'er had a king until his time.
Virtue he had, deserving to command:
His brandish'd sword did blind men with his beams:
His arms spread wider than a dragon's wings;
His sparking eyes, replete with wrathful fire,
More dazzled and drove back his enemies
Than mid-day sun fierce bent against their faces.
What should I say? his deeds exceed all speech:
He ne'er lift up his hand but conquered.

EXETER

We mourn in black: why mourn we not in blood?
Henry is dead and never shall revive:
Upon a wooden coffin we attend,
And death's dishonourable victory
We with our stately presence glorify,
Like captives bound to a triumphant car.
What! shall we curse the planets of mishap
That plotted thus our glory's overthrow?
Or shall we think the subtle-witted French
Conjurers and sorcerers, that afraid of him
By magic verses have contrived his end?
BISHOP

OF WINCHESTER

He was a king bless'd of the King of kings.
Unto the French the dreadful judgement-day
So dreadful will not be as was his sight.
The battles of the Lord of hosts he fought:
The church's prayers made him so prosperous.

GLOUCESTER

The church! where is it? Had not churchmen pray'd,
His thread of life had not so soon decay'd:
None do you like but an effeminate prince,
Whom, like a school-boy, you may over-awe.
BISHOP

OF WINCHESTER

Gloucester, whate'er we like, thou art protector
And lookest to command the prince and realm.
Thy wife is proud; she holdeth thee in awe,
More than God or religious churchmen may.

GLOUCESTER

Name not religion, for thou lovest the flesh,
And ne'er throughout the year to church thou go'st
Except it be to pray against thy foes.

BEDFORD

Cease, cease these jars and rest your minds in peace:
Let's to the altar: heralds, wait on us:
Instead of gold, we'll offer up our arms:
Since arms avail not now that Henry's dead.
Posterity, await for wretched years,
When at their mothers' moist eyes babes shall suck,
Our isle be made a nourish of salt tears,
And none but women left to wail the dead.
Henry the Fifth, thy ghost I invocate:
Prosper this realm, keep it from civil broils,
Combat with adverse planets in the heavens!
A far more glorious star thy soul will make
Than Julius Caesar or bright--

Enter a Messenger

Messenger

My honourable lords, health to you all!
Sad tidings bring I to you out of France,
Of loss, of slaughter and discomfiture:
Guienne, Champagne, Rheims, Orleans,
Paris, Guysors, Poictiers, are all quite lost.

BEDFORD

What say'st thou, man, before dead Henry's corse?
Speak softly, or the loss of those great towns
Will make him burst his lead and rise from death.

GLOUCESTER

Is Paris lost? is Rouen yielded up?
If Henry were recall'd to life again,
These news would cause him once more yield the ghost.

EXETER

How were they lost? what treachery was used?

Messenger

No treachery; but want of men and money.
Amongst the soldiers this is muttered,

That here you maintain several factions,
And whilst a field should be dispatch'd and fought,
You are disputing of your generals:
One would have lingering wars with little cost;
Another would fly swift, but wanteth wings;
A third thinks, without expense at all,
By guileful fair words peace may be obtain'd.
Awake, awake, English nobility!
Let not sloth dim your horrors new-begot:
Cropp'd are the flower-de-luces in your arms;
Of England's coat one half is cut away.

EXETER

Were our tears wanting to this funeral,
These tidings would call forth their flowing tides.

BEDFORD

Me they concern; Regent I am of France.
Give me my steeled coat. I'll fight for France.
Away with these disgraceful wailing robes!
Wounds will I lend the French instead of eyes,
To weep their intermissive miseries.

Enter to them another Messenger

Messenger

Lords, view these letters full of bad mischance.
France is revolted from the English quite,
Except some petty towns of no import:
The Dauphin Charles is crowned king of Rheims;
The Bastard of Orleans with him is join'd;
Reignier, Duke of Anjou, doth take his part;
The Duke of Alencon flieth to his side.

EXETER

The Dauphin crowned king! all fly to him!
O, whither shall we fly from this reproach?

GLOUCESTER

We will not fly, but to our enemies' throats.
Bedford, if thou be slack, I'll fight it out.

BEDFORD

Gloucester, why doubt'st thou of my forwardness?
An army have I muster'd in my thoughts,
Wherewith already France is overrun.

Enter another Messenger

Messenger

My gracious lords, to add to your laments,
Wherewith you now bedew King Henry's hearse,
I must inform you of a dismal fight
Betwixt the stout Lord Talbot and the French.
BISHOP

OF WINCHESTER

What! wherein Talbot overcame? is't so?

Messenger

O, no; wherein Lord Talbot was o'erthrown:
The circumstance I'll tell you more at large.
The tenth of August last this dreadful lord,
Retiring from the siege of Orleans,
Having full scarce six thousand in his troop.
By three and twenty thousand of the French
Was round encompassed and set upon.
No leisure had he to enrank his men;
He wanted pikes to set before his archers;
Instead whereof sharp stakes pluck'd out of hedges
They pitched in the ground confusedly,
To keep the horsemen off from breaking in.
More than three hours the fight continued;
Where valiant Talbot above human thought
Enacted wonders with his sword and lance:
Hundreds he sent to hell, and none durst stand him;
Here, there, and every where, enraged he flew:

The French exclaim'd, the devil was in arms;
All the whole army stood agazed on him:
His soldiers spying his undaunted spirit
A Talbot! a Talbot! cried out amain
And rush'd into the bowels of the battle.
Here had the conquest fully been seal'd up,
If Sir John Fastolfe had not play'd the coward:
He, being in the vaward, placed behind
With purpose to relieve and follow them,
Cowardly fled, not having struck one stroke.
Hence grew the general wreck and massacre;
Enclosed were they with their enemies:
A base Walloon, to win the Dauphin's grace,
Thrust Talbot with a spear into the back,
Whom all France with their chief assembled strength
Durst not presume to look once in the face.

BEDFORD

Is Talbot slain? then I will slay myself,
For living idly here in pomp and ease,
Whilst such a worthy leader, wanting aid,
Unto his dastard foemen is betray'd.

Messenger

O no, he lives; but is took prisoner,
And Lord Scales with him and Lord Hungerford:
Most of the rest slaughter'd or took likewise.

BEDFORD

His ransom there is none but I shall pay:
I'll hale the Dauphin headlong from his throne:
His crown shall be the ransom of my friend;
Four of their lords I'll change for one of ours.
Farewell, my masters; to my task will I;
Bonfires in France forthwith I am to make,
To keep our great Saint George's feast withal:
Ten thousand soldiers with me I will take,
Whose bloody deeds shall make all Europe quake.

Messenger

So you had need; for Orleans is besieged;
The English army is grown weak and faint:
The Earl of Salisbury craveth supply,
And hardly keeps his men from mutiny,
Since they, so few, watch such a multitude.

EXETER

Remember, lords, your oaths to Henry sworn,
Either to quell the Dauphin utterly,
Or bring him in obedience to your yoke.

BEDFORD

I do remember it; and here take my leave,
To go about my preparation.

Exit

GLOUCESTER

I'll to the Tower with all the haste I can,
To view the artillery and munition;
And then I will proclaim young Henry king.

Exit

EXETER

To Eltham will I, where the young king is,
Being ordain'd his special governor,
And for his safety there I'll best devise.

Exit

BISHOP

OF WINCHESTER

Each hath his place and function to attend:
I am left out; for me nothing remains.
But long I will not be Jack out of office:
The king from Eltham I intend to steal
And sit at chiefest stern of public weal.

Exeunt

SCENE II. France. Before Orleans.

Sound a flourish. Enter CHARLES, ALENCON, and REIGNIER, marching with drum and Soldiers

CHARLES

Mars his true moving, even as in the heavens
So in the earth, to this day is not known:
Late did he shine upon the English side;
Now we are victors; upon us he smiles.
What towns of any moment but we have?
At pleasure here we lie near Orleans;
Otherwhiles the famish'd English, like pale ghosts,
Faintly besiege us one hour in a month.

ALENCON

They want their porridge and their fat bull-beeves:
Either they must be dieted like mules
And have their provender tied to their mouths
Or piteous they will look, like drowned mice.

REIGNIER

Let's raise the siege: why live we idly here?
Talbot is taken, whom we wont to fear:
Remaineth none but mad-brain'd Salisbury;
And he may well in fretting spend his gall,
Nor men nor money hath he to make war.

CHARLES

Sound, sound alarum! we will rush on them.
Now for the honour of the forlorn French!
Him I forgive my death that killeth me
When he sees me go back one foot or fly.

Exeunt

Here alarum; they are beaten back by the English with great loss.
Re-enter CHARLES, ALENCON, and REIGNIER

CHARLES

Who ever saw the like? what men have I!
Dogs! cowards! dastards! I would ne'er have fled,
But that they left me 'midst my enemies.

REIGNIER

Salisbury is a desperate homicide;
He fighteth as one weary of his life.
The other lords, like lions wanting food,
Do rush upon us as their hungry prey.

ALENCON

Froissart, a countryman of ours, records,
England all Olivers and Rowlands bred,
During the time Edward the Third did reign.
More truly now may this be verified;
For none but Samsons and Goliases
It sendeth forth to skirmish. One to ten!
Lean, raw-boned rascals! who would e'er suppose
They had such courage and audacity?

CHARLES

Let's leave this town; for they are hare-brain'd slaves,
And hunger will enforce them to be more eager:
Of old I know them; rather with their teeth
The walls they'll tear down than forsake the siege.

REIGNIER

I think, by some odd gimmors or device
Their arms are set like clocks, stiff to strike on;
Else ne'er could they hold out so as they do.
By my consent, we'll even let them alone.

ALENCON

Be it so.

Enter the BASTARD OF ORLEANS

BASTARD OF ORLEANS

Where's the Prince Dauphin? I have news for him.

CHARLES

Bastard of Orleans, thrice welcome to us.

BASTARD OF ORLEANS

Methinks your looks are sad, your cheer appall'd:
Hath the late overthrow wrought this offence?
Be not dismay'd, for succor is at hand:
A holy maid hither with me I bring,
Which by a vision sent to her from heaven
Ordained is to raise this tedious siege
And drive the English forth the bounds of France.
The spirit of deep prophecy she hath,
Exceeding the nine sibyls of old Rome:
What's past and what's to come she can descry.
Speak, shall I call her in? Believe my words,
For they are certain and unfallible.

CHARLES

Go, call her in.

Exit BASTARD OF ORLEANS

But first, to try her skill,
Reignier, stand thou as Dauphin in my place:
Question her proudly; let thy looks be stern:
By this means shall we sound what skill she hath.

Re-enter the BASTARD OF ORLEANS, with JOAN LA PUCELLE

REIGNIER

Fair maid, is't thou wilt do these wondrous feats?

JOAN LA PUCELLE

Reignier, is't thou that thinkest to beguile me?
Where is the Dauphin? Come, come from behind;
I know thee well, though never seen before.
Be not amazed, there's nothing hid from me:
In private will I talk with thee apart.
Stand back, you lords, and give us leave awhile.

REIGNIER

She takes upon her bravely at first dash.

JOAN LA PUCELLE

Dauphin, I am by birth a shepherd's daughter,
My wit untrain'd in any kind of art.
Heaven and our Lady gracious hath it pleased
To shine on my contemptible estate:
Lo, whilst I waited on my tender lambs,
And to sun's parching heat display'd my cheeks,
God's mother deigned to appear to me
And in a vision full of majesty
Will'd me to leave my base vocation
And free my country from calamity:
Her aid she promised and assured success:
In complete glory she reveal'd herself;
And, whereas I was black and swart before,
With those clear rays which she infused on me
That beauty am I bless'd with which you see.
Ask me what question thou canst possible,
And I will answer unpremeditated:
My courage try by combat, if thou darest,
And thou shalt find that I exceed my sex.
Resolve on this, thou shalt be fortunate,
If thou receive me for thy warlike mate.

CHARLES

Thou hast astonish'd me with thy high terms:
Only this proof I'll of thy valour make,
In single combat thou shalt buckle with me,
And if thou vanquishest, thy words are true;
Otherwise I renounce all confidence.

JOAN LA PUCELLE

I am prepared: here is my keen-edged sword,
Deck'd with five flower-de-luces on each side;
The which at Touraine, in Saint Katharine's
churchyard,
Out of a great deal of old iron I chose forth.

CHARLES

Then come, o' God's name; I fear no woman.

JOAN LA PUCELLE

And while I live, I'll ne'er fly from a man.

Here they fight, and JOAN LA PUCELLE overcomes

CHARLES

Stay, stay thy hands! thou art an Amazon
And fightest with the sword of Deborah.

JOAN LA PUCELLE

Christ's mother helps me, else I were too weak.

CHARLES

Whoe'er helps thee, 'tis thou that must help me:
Impatiently I burn with thy desire;
My heart and hands thou hast at once subdued.
Excellent Pucelle, if thy name be so,
Let me thy servant and not sovereign be:
'Tis the French Dauphin sueth to thee thus.

JOAN LA PUCELLE

I must not yield to any rites of love,
For my profession's sacred from above:
When I have chased all thy foes from hence,
Then will I think upon a recompense.

CHARLES

Meantime look gracious on thy prostrate thrall.

REIGNIER

My lord, methinks, is very long in talk.

ALENCON

Doubtless he shrives this woman to her smock;
Else ne'er could he so long protract his speech.

REIGNIER

Shall we disturb him, since he keeps no mean?

ALENCON

He may mean more than we poor men do know:
These women are shrewd tempters with their tongues.

REIGNIER

My lord, where are you? what devise you on?
Shall we give over Orleans, or no?

JOAN LA PUCELLE

Why, no, I say, distrustful recreants!
Fight till the last gasp; I will be your guard.

CHARLES

What she says I'll confirm: we'll fight it out.

JOAN LA PUCELLE

Assign'd am I to be the English scourge.
This night the siege assuredly I'll raise:
Expect Saint Martin's summer, halcyon days,
Since I have entered into these wars.
Glory is like a circle in the water,
Which never ceaseth to enlarge itself
Till by broad spreading it disperse to nought.
With Henry's death the English circle ends;
Dispersed are the glories it included.
Now am I like that proud insulting ship
Which Caesar and his fortune bare at once.

CHARLES

Was Mahomet inspired with a dove?
Thou with an eagle art inspired then.
Helen, the mother of great Constantine,
Nor yet Saint Philip's daughters, were like thee.
Bright star of Venus, fall'n down on the earth,
How may I reverently worship thee enough?

ALENCON

Leave off delays, and let us raise the siege.

REIGNIER

Woman, do what thou canst to save our honours;
Drive them from Orleans and be immortalized.

CHARLES

Presently we'll try: come, let's away about it:
No prophet will I trust, if she prove false.

Exeunt

SCENE III. London. Before the Tower.

Enter GLOUCESTER, with his Serving-men in blue coats

GLOUCESTER

I am come to survey the Tower this day:
Since Henry's death, I fear, there is conveyance.
Where be these warders, that they wait not here?
Open the gates; 'tis Gloucester that calls.

First Warder

[Within] Who's there that knocks so imperiously?
First Serving-Man It is the noble Duke of Gloucester.

Second Warder

[Within] Whoe'er he be, you may not be let in.
First Serving-Man Villains, answer you so the lord protector?

First Warder

[Within] The Lord protect him! so we answer him:
We do no otherwise than we are will'd.

GLOUCESTER

Who willed you? or whose will stands but mine?
There's none protector of the realm but I.
Break up the gates, I'll be your warrantize.
Shall I be flouted thus by dunghill grooms?

Gloucester's men rush at the Tower Gates, and WOODVILE the
Lieutenant speaks within

WOODVILE

What noise is this? what traitors have we here?

GLOUCESTER

Lieutenant, is it you whose voice I hear?
Open the gates; here's Gloucester that would enter.

WOODVILE

Have patience, noble duke; I may not open;
The Cardinal of Winchester forbids:
From him I have express commandment
That thou nor none of thine shall be let in.

GLOUCESTER

Faint-hearted Woodvile, prizest him 'fore me?
Arrogant Winchester, that haughty prelate,
Whom Henry, our late sovereign, ne'er could brook?
Thou art no friend to God or to the king:
Open the gates, or I'll shut thee out shortly.
Serving-Men Open the gates unto the lord protector,
Or we'll burst them open, if that you come not quickly.

Enter to the Protector at the Tower Gates BISHOP OF WINCHESTER
and his men in tawny coats

BISHOP

OF WINCHESTER

How now, ambitious Humphry! what means this?

GLOUCESTER

Peel'd priest, dost thou command me to be shut out?
BISHOP

OF WINCHESTER

I do, thou most usurping proditor,
And not protector, of the king or realm.

GLOUCESTER

Stand back, thou manifest conspirator,
Thou that contrivedst to murder our dead lord;
Thou that givest whores indulgences to sin:
I'll canvass thee in thy broad cardinal's hat,

If thou proceed in this thy insolence.

BISHOP

OF WINCHESTER

Nay, stand thou back, I will not budge a foot:
This be Damascus, be thou cursed Cain,
To slay thy brother Abel, if thou wilt.

GLOUCESTER

I will not slay thee, but I'll drive thee back:
Thy scarlet robes as a child's bearing-cloth
I'll use to carry thee out of this place.

BISHOP

OF WINCHESTER

Do what thou darest; I beard thee to thy face.

GLOUCESTER

What! am I dared and bearded to my face?
Draw, men, for all this privileged place;
Blue coats to tawny coats. Priest, beware your beard,
I mean to tug it and to cuff you soundly:
Under my feet I stamp thy cardinal's hat:
In spite of pope or dignities of church,
Here by the cheeks I'll drag thee up and down.

BISHOP

OF WINCHESTER

Gloucester, thou wilt answer this before the pope.

GLOUCESTER

Winchester goose, I cry, a rope! a rope!
Now beat them hence; why do you let them stay?
Thee I'll chase hence, thou wolf in sheep's array.
Out, tawny coats! out, scarlet hypocrite!

Here GLOUCESTER's men beat out BISHOP OF WINCHESTER's men,
and enter in the hurly- burly the Mayor of London and his Officers

Mayor

Fie, lords! that you, being supreme magistrates,
Thus contumeliously should break the peace!

GLOUCESTER

Peace, mayor! thou know'st little of my wrongs:
Here's Beaufort, that regards nor God nor king,
Hath here distrain'd the Tower to his use.
BISHOP

OF WINCHESTER

Here's Gloucester, a foe to citizens,
One that still motions war and never peace,
O'ercharging your free purses with large fines,
That seeks to overthrow religion,
Because he is protector of the realm,
And would have armour here out of the Tower,
To crown himself king and suppress the prince.

GLOUCESTER

I will not answer thee with words, but blows.

Here they skirmish again

Mayor

Naught rests for me in this tumultuous strife
But to make open proclamation:
Come, officer; as loud as e'er thou canst,
Cry.

Officer

All manner of men assembled here in arms this day
against God's peace and the king's, we charge and
command you, in his highness' name, to repair to
your several dwelling-places; and not to wear,
handle, or use any sword, weapon, or dagger,
henceforward, upon pain of death.

GLOUCESTER

Cardinal, I'll be no breaker of the law:
But we shall meet, and break our minds at large.
BISHOP

OF WINCHESTER

Gloucester, we will meet; to thy cost, be sure:
Thy heart-blood I will have for this day's work.

Mayor

I'll call for clubs, if you will not away.
This cardinal's more haughty than the devil.

GLOUCESTER

Mayor, farewell: thou dost but what thou mayst.
BISHOP

OF WINCHESTER

Abominable Gloucester, guard thy head;
For I intend to have it ere long.

Exeunt, severally, GLOUCESTER and BISHOP OF WINCHESTER with their Serving-men

Mayor

See the coast clear'd, and then we will depart.
Good God, these nobles should such stomachs bear!
I myself fight not once in forty year.

Exeunt

SCENE IV. Orleans.

Enter, on the walls, a Master Gunner and his Boy

Master-Gunner Sirrah, thou know'st how Orleans is besieged,
And how the English have the suburbs won.

Boy

Father, I know; and oft have shot at them,
Howe'er unfortunate I miss'd my aim.
Master-Gunner But now thou shalt not. Be thou ruled by me:
Chief master-gunner am I of this town;
Something I must do to procure me grace.
The prince's espials have informed me
How the English, in the suburbs close intrench'd,
Wont, through a secret grate of iron bars
In yonder tower, to overpeer the city,
And thence discover how with most advantage
They may vex us with shot, or with assault.
To intercept this inconvenience,

A piece of ordnance 'gainst it I have placed;
And even these three days have I watch'd,
If I could see them.
Now do thou watch, for I can stay no longer.
If thou spy'st any, run and bring me word;
And thou shalt find me at the governor's.

Exit

Boy

Father, I warrant you; take you no care;
I'll never trouble you, if I may spy them.

Exit

Enter, on the turrets, SALISBURY and TALBOT, GLANSDALE,
GARGRAVE, and others

SALISBURY

Talbot, my life, my joy, again return'd!
How wert thou handled being prisoner?
Or by what means got'st thou to be released?
Discourse, I prithee, on this turret's top.

TALBOT

The Duke of Bedford had a prisoner
Call'd the brave Lord Ponton de Santrailles;
For him was I exchanged and ransomed.
But with a baser man of arms by far
Once in contempt they would have barter'd me:
Which I, disdaining, scorn'd; and craved death,
Rather than I would be so vile esteem'd.
In fine, redeem'd I was as I desired.
But, O! the treacherous Fastolfe wounds my heart,
Whom with my bare fists I would execute,
If I now had him brought into my power.

SALISBURY

Yet tell'st thou not how thou wert entertain'd.

TALBOT

With scoffs and scorns and contumelious taunts.
In open market-place produced they me,

To be a public spectacle to all:
Here, said they, is the terror of the French,
The scarecrow that affrights our children so.
Then broke I from the officers that led me,
And with my nails digg'd stones out of the ground,
To hurl at the beholders of my shame:
My grisly countenance made others fly;
None durst come near for fear of sudden death.
In iron walls they deem'd me not secure;
So great fear of my name 'mongst them was spread,
That they supposed I could rend bars of steel,
And spurn in pieces posts of adamant:
Wherefore a guard of chosen shot I had,
That walked about me every minute-while;
And if I did but stir out of my bed,
Ready they were to shoot me to the heart.

Enter the Boy with a linstock

SALISBURY

I grieve to hear what torments you endured,
But we will be revenged sufficiently
Now it is supper-time in Orleans:
Here, through this grate, I count each one
and view the Frenchmen how they fortify:
Let us look in; the sight will much delight thee.
Sir Thomas Gargrave, and Sir William Glansdale,
Let me have your express opinions
Where is best place to make our battery next.

GARGRAVE

I think, at the north gate; for there stand lords.

GLANSDALE

And I, here, at the bulwark of the bridge.

TALBOT

For aught I see, this city must be famish'd,
Or with light skirmishes enfeebled.

Here they shoot. SALISBURY and GARGRAVE fall

SALISBURY

O Lord, have mercy on us, wretched sinners!

GARGRAVE

O Lord, have mercy on me, woful man!

TALBOT

What chance is this that suddenly hath cross'd us?
Speak, Salisbury; at least, if thou canst speak:
How farest thou, mirror of all martial men?
One of thy eyes and thy cheek's side struck off!
Accursed tower! accursed fatal hand
That hath contrived this woful tragedy!
In thirteen battles Salisbury o'ercame;
Henry the Fifth he first train'd to the wars;
Whilst any trump did sound, or drum struck up,
His sword did ne'er leave striking in the field.
Yet livest thou, Salisbury? though thy speech doth fail,
One eye thou hast, to look to heaven for grace:
The sun with one eye vieweth all the world.
Heaven, be thou gracious to none alive,
If Salisbury wants mercy at thy hands!
Bear hence his body; I will help to bury it.
Sir Thomas Gargrave, hast thou any life?
Speak unto Talbot; nay, look up to him.
Salisbury, cheer thy spirit with this comfort;
Thou shalt not die whiles--
He beckons with his hand and smiles on me.
As who should say 'When I am dead and gone,
Remember to avenge me on the French.'
Plantagenet, I will; and like thee, Nero,
Play on the lute, beholding the towns burn:
Wretched shall France be only in my name.

Here an alarum, and it thunders and lightens

What stir is this? what tumult's in the heavens?
Whence cometh this alarum and the noise?

Enter a Messenger

Henry VI – Part I

Messenger

My lord, my lord, the French have gathered head:
The Dauphin, with one Joan la Pucelle join'd,
A holy prophetess new risen up,
Is come with a great power to raise the siege.

Here SALISBURY lifteth himself up and groans

TALBOT

Hear, hear how dying Salisbury doth groan!
It irks his heart he cannot be revenged.
Frenchmen, I'll be a Salisbury to you:
Pucelle or puzzel, dolphin or dogfish,
Your hearts I'll stamp out with my horse's heels,
And make a quagmire of your mingled brains.
Convey me Salisbury into his tent,
And then we'll try what these dastard Frenchmen dare.

Alarum. Exeunt

SCENE V. The same.

*Here an alarum again: and TALBOT pursueth the DAUPHIN, and
driveth him: then enter JOAN LA PUCELLE, driving Englishmen before
her, and exit after them then re-enter TALBOT*

TALBOT

Where is my strength, my valour, and my force?
Our English troops retire, I cannot stay them:
A woman clad in armour chaseth them.

Re-enter JOAN LA PUCELLE

Here, here she comes. I'll have a bout with thee;
Devil or devil's dam, I'll conjure thee:
Blood will I draw on thee, thou art a witch,
And straightway give thy soul to him thou servest.

JOAN LA PUCELLE

Come, come, 'tis only I that must disgrace thee.

Here they fight

TALBOT

Heavens, can you suffer hell so to prevail?
My breast I'll burst with straining of my courage
And from my shoulders crack my arms asunder.
But I will chastise this high-minded strumpet.

They fight again

JOAN LA PUCELLE

Talbot, farewell; thy hour is not yet come:
I must go victual Orleans forthwith.

A short alarum; then enter the town with soldiers

O'ertake me, if thou canst; I scorn thy strength.
Go, go, cheer up thy hungry-starved men;
Help Salisbury to make his testament:
This day is ours, as many more shall be.

Exit

TALBOT

My thoughts are whirled like a potter's wheel;
I know not where I am, nor what I do;
A witch, by fear, not force, like Hannibal,
Drives back our troops and conquers as she lists:
So bees with smoke and doves with noisome stench
Are from their hives and houses driven away.
They call'd us for our fierceness English dogs;
Now, like to whelps, we crying run away.

A short alarum

Hark, countrymen! either renew the fight,
Or tear the lions out of England's coat;
Renounce your soil, give sheep in lions' stead:
Sheep run not half so treacherous from the wolf,
Or horse or oxen from the leopard,
As you fly from your oft-subdued slaves.

Alarum. Here another skirmish

It will not be: retire into your trenches:
You all consented unto Salisbury's death,

For none would strike a stroke in his revenge.
Pucelle is enter'd into Orleans,
In spite of us or aught that we could do.
O, would I were to die with Salisbury!
The shame hereof will make me hide my head.

Exit TALBOT. Alarum; retreat; flourish

SCENE VI. The same.

Enter, on the walls, JOAN LA PUCELLE, CHARLES, REIGNIER, ALENCON, and Soldiers

JOAN LA PUCELLE

Advance our waving colours on the walls;
Rescued is Orleans from the English
Thus Joan la Pucelle hath perform'd her word.

CHARLES

Divinest creature, Astraea's daughter,
How shall I honour thee for this success?
Thy promises are like Adonis' gardens
That one day bloom'd and fruitful were the next.
France, triumph in thy glorious prophetess!
Recover'd is the town of Orleans:
More blessed hap did ne'er befall our state.

REIGNIER

Why ring not out the bells aloud throughout the town?
Dauphin, command the citizens make bonfires
And feast and banquet in the open streets,
To celebrate the joy that God hath given us.

ALENCON

All France will be replete with mirth and joy,
When they shall hear how we have play'd the men.

CHARLES

'Tis Joan, not we, by whom the day is won;
For which I will divide my crown with her,
And all the priests and friars in my realm

Shall in procession sing her endless praise.
A statelier pyramis to her I'll rear
Than Rhodope's or Memphis' ever was:
In memory of her when she is dead,
Her ashes, in an urn more precious
Than the rich-jewel'd of Darius,
Transported shall be at high festivals
Before the kings and queens of France.
No longer on Saint Denis will we cry,
But Joan la Pucelle shall be France's saint.
Come in, and let us banquet royally,
After this golden day of victory.

Flourish. Exeunt

ACT II

SCENE I. Before Orleans.

Enter a Sergeant of a band with two Sentinels

Sergeant

Sirs, take your places and be vigilant:
If any noise or soldier you perceive
Near to the walls, by some apparent sign
Let us have knowledge at the court of guard.

First Sentinel

Sergeant, you shall.

Exit Sergeant

Thus are poor servitors,
When others sleep upon their quiet beds,
Constrain'd to watch in darkness, rain and cold.

Enter TALBOT, BEDFORD, BURGUNDY, and Forces, with scaling-ladders, their drums beating a dead march

TALBOT

Lord Regent, and redoubted Burgundy,
By whose approach the regions of Artois,
Wallon and Picardy are friends to us,
This happy night the Frenchmen are secure,
Having all day caroused and banqueted:
Embrace we then this opportunity
As fitting best to quittance their deceit
Contrived by art and baleful sorcery.

BEDFORD

Coward of France! how much he wrongs his fame,
Despairing of his own arm's fortitude,
To join with witches and the help of hell!

BURGUNDY

Traitors have never other company.
But what's that Pucelle whom they term so pure?

TALBOT

A maid, they say.

BEDFORD

A maid! and be so martial!

BURGUNDY

Pray God she prove not masculine ere long,
If underneath the standard of the French
She carry armour as she hath begun.

TALBOT

Well, let them practise and converse with spirits:
God is our fortress, in whose conquering name
Let us resolve to scale their flinty bulwarks.

BEDFORD

Ascend, brave Talbot; we will follow thee.

TALBOT

Not all together: better far, I guess,
That we do make our entrance several ways;
That, if it chance the one of us do fail,
The other yet may rise against their force.

BEDFORD

Agreed: I'll to yond corner.

BURGUNDY

And I to this.

TALBOT

And here will Talbot mount, or make his grave.
Now, Salisbury, for thee, and for the right

Of English Henry, shall this night appear
How much in duty I am bound to both.

Sentinels

Arm! arm! the enemy doth make assault!

Cry: 'St. George,' 'A Talbot.'

The French leap over the walls in their shirts. Enter, several ways, the BASTARD OF ORLEANS, ALENCON, and REIGNIER, half ready, and half unready

ALENCON

How now, my lords! what, all unready so?

BASTARD OF ORLEANS

Unready! ay, and glad we 'scaped so well.

REIGNIER

'Twas time, I trow, to wake and leave our beds,
Hearing alarums at our chamber-doors.

ALENCON

Of all exploits since first I follow'd arms,
Ne'er heard I of a warlike enterprise
More venturous or desperate than this.

BASTARD OF ORLEANS

I think this Talbot be a fiend of hell.

REIGNIER

If not of hell, the heavens, sure, favour him.

ALENCON

Here cometh Charles: I marvel how he sped.

BASTARD OF ORLEANS

Tut, holy Joan was his defensive guard.

Enter CHARLES and JOAN LA PUCELLE

CHARLES

Is this thy cunning, thou deceitful dame?
Didst thou at first, to flatter us withal,

Make us partakers of a little gain,
That now our loss might be ten times so much?

JOAN LA PUCELLE

Wherefore is Charles impatient with his friend!
At all times will you have my power alike?
Sleeping or waking must I still prevail,
Or will you blame and lay the fault on me?
Improvident soldiers! had your watch been good,
This sudden mischief never could have fall'n.

CHARLES

Duke of Alencon, this was your default,
That, being captain of the watch to-night,
Did look no better to that weighty charge.

ALENCON

Had all your quarters been as safely kept
As that whereof I had the government,
We had not been thus shamefully surprised.

BASTARD OF ORLEANS

Mine was secure.

REIGNIER

And so was mine, my lord.

CHARLES

And, for myself, most part of all this night,
Within her quarter and mine own precinct
I was employ'd in passing to and fro,
About relieving of the sentinels:
Then how or which way should they first break in?

JOAN LA PUCELLE

Question, my lords, no further of the case,
How or which way: 'tis sure they found some place
But weakly guarded, where the breach was made.
And now there rests no other shift but this;
To gather our soldiers, scatter'd and dispersed,
And lay new platforms to endamage them.

Henry VI – Part I

Alarum. Enter an English Soldier, crying 'A Talbot! a Talbot!' They fly, leaving their clothes behind

Soldier

I'll be so bold to take what they have left.
The cry of Talbot serves me for a sword;
For I have loaden me with many spoils,
Using no other weapon but his name.

Exit

SCENE II. Orleans. Within the town.

Enter TALBOT, BEDFORD, BURGUNDY, a Captain, and others

BEDFORD

The day begins to break, and night is fled,
Whose pitchy mantle over-veil'd the earth.
Here sound retreat, and cease our hot pursuit.

Retreat sounded

TALBOT

Bring forth the body of old Salisbury,
And here advance it in the market-place,
The middle centre of this cursed town.
Now have I paid my vow unto his soul;
For every drop of blood was drawn from him,
There hath at least five Frenchmen died tonight.
And that hereafter ages may behold
What ruin happen'd in revenge of him,
Within their chiefest temple I'll erect
A tomb, wherein his corpse shall be interr'd:
Upon the which, that every one may read,
Shall be engraved the sack of Orleans,
The treacherous manner of his mournful death
And what a terror he had been to France.
But, lords, in all our bloody massacre,
I muse we met not with the Dauphin's grace,
His new-come champion, virtuous Joan of Arc,
Nor any of his false confederates.

BEDFORD

'Tis thought, Lord Talbot, when the fight began,
Roused on the sudden from their drowsy beds,
They did amongst the troops of armed men
Leap o'er the walls for refuge in the field.

BURGUNDY

Myself, as far as I could well discern
For smoke and dusky vapours of the night,
Am sure I scared the Dauphin and his trull,
When arm in arm they both came swiftly running,
Like to a pair of loving turtle-doves
That could not live asunder day or night.
After that things are set in order here,
We'll follow them with all the power we have.

Enter a Messenger

Messenger

All hail, my lords! which of this princely train
Call ye the warlike Talbot, for his acts
So much applauded through the realm of France?

TALBOT

Here is the Talbot: who would speak with him?

Messenger

The virtuous lady, Countess of Auvergne,
With modesty admiring thy renown,
By me entreats, great lord, thou wouldst vouchsafe
To visit her poor castle where she lies,
That she may boast she hath beheld the man
Whose glory fills the world with loud report.

BURGUNDY

Is it even so? Nay, then, I see our wars
Will turn unto a peaceful comic sport,
When ladies crave to be encounter'd with.
You may not, my lord, despise her gentle suit.

TALBOT

Ne'er trust me then; for when a world of men
Could not prevail with all their oratory,
Yet hath a woman's kindness over-ruled:
And therefore tell her I return great thanks,
And in submission will attend on her.
Will not your honours bear me company?

BEDFORD

No, truly; it is more than manners will:
And I have heard it said, unbidden guests
Are often welcomest when they are gone.

TALBOT

Well then, alone, since there's no remedy,
I mean to prove this lady's courtesy.
Come hither, captain.

Whispers

You perceive my mind?

Captain

I do, my lord, and mean accordingly.

Exeunt

SCENE III. Auvergne. The COUNTESS's castle.

Enter the COUNTESS and her Porter

COUNTESS

OF AUVERGNE

Porter, remember what I gave in charge;
And when you have done so, bring the keys to me.

Porter

Madam, I will.

Exit

COUNTESS

OF AUVERGNE

The plot is laid: if all things fall out right,
I shall as famous be by this exploit
As Scythian Tomyris by Cyrus' death.
Great is the rumor of this dreadful knight,
And his achievements of no less account:
Fain would mine eyes be witness with mine ears,
To give their censure of these rare reports.

Enter Messenger and TALBOT

Messenger

Madam,
According as your ladyship desired,
By message craved, so is Lord Talbot come.
COUNTESS

OF AUVERGNE

And he is welcome. What! is this the man?

Messenger

Madam, it is.
COUNTESS

OF AUVERGNE

Is this the scourge of France?
Is this the Talbot, so much fear'd abroad
That with his name the mothers still their babes?
I see report is fabulous and false:
I thought I should have seen some Hercules,
A second Hector, for his grim aspect,
And large proportion of his strong-knit limbs.
Alas, this is a child, a silly dwarf!
It cannot be this weak and writhled shrimp
Should strike such terror to his enemies.

TALBOT

Madam, I have been bold to trouble you;
But since your ladyship is not at leisure,

I'll sort some other time to visit you.

COUNTESS

OF AUVERGNE

What means he now? Go ask him whither he goes.

Messenger

Stay, my Lord Talbot; for my lady craves
To know the cause of your abrupt departure.

TALBOT

Marry, for that she's in a wrong belief,
I go to certify her Talbot's here.

Re-enter Porter with keys

COUNTESS

OF AUVERGNE

If thou be he, then art thou prisoner.

TALBOT

Prisoner! to whom?

COUNTESS

OF AUVERGNE

To me, blood-thirsty lord;
And for that cause I trained thee to my house.
Long time thy shadow hath been thrall to me,
For in my gallery thy picture hangs:
But now the substance shall endure the like,
And I will chain these legs and arms of thine,
That hast by tyranny these many years
Wasted our country, slain our citizens
And sent our sons and husbands captivate.

TALBOT

Ha, ha, ha!

COUNTESS

OF AUVERGNE

Laughest thou, wretch? thy mirth shall turn to moan.

TALBOT

I laugh to see your ladyship so fond
To think that you have aught but Talbot's shadow
Whereon to practise your severity.

COUNTESS

OF AUVERGNE

Why, art not thou the man?

TALBOT

I am indeed.

COUNTESS

OF AUVERGNE

Then have I substance too.

TALBOT

No, no, I am but shadow of myself:
You are deceived, my substance is not here;
For what you see is but the smallest part
And least proportion of humanity:
I tell you, madam, were the whole frame here,
It is of such a spacious lofty pitch,
Your roof were not sufficient to contain't.

COUNTESS

OF AUVERGNE

This is a riddling merchant for the nonce;
He will be here, and yet he is not here:
How can these contrarieties agree?

TALBOT

That will I show you presently.

Winds his horn. Drums strike up: a peal of ordnance. Enter soldiers

How say you, madam? are you now persuaded
That Talbot is but shadow of himself?
These are his substance, sinews, arms and strength,
With which he yoketh your rebellious necks,
Razeth your cities and subverts your towns

And in a moment makes them desolate.

COUNTESS

OF AUVERGNE

Victorious Talbot! pardon my abuse:
I find thou art no less than fame hath bruited
And more than may be gather'd by thy shape.
Let my presumption not provoke thy wrath;
For I am sorry that with reverence
I did not entertain thee as thou art.

TALBOT

Be not dismay'd, fair lady; nor misconstrue
The mind of Talbot, as you did mistake
The outward composition of his body.
What you have done hath not offended me;
Nor other satisfaction do I crave,
But only, with your patience, that we may
Taste of your wine and see what cates you have;
For soldiers' stomachs always serve them well.

COUNTESS

OF AUVERGNE

With all my heart, and think me honoured
To feast so great a warrior in my house.

Exeunt

SCENE IV. London. The Temple-garden.

*Enter the Earls of SOMERSET, SUFFOLK, and WARWICK; RICHARD
PLANTAGENET, VERNON, and another Lawyer*

RICHARD

PLANTAGENET

Great lords and gentlemen, what means this silence?
Dare no man answer in a case of truth?

SUFFOLK

Within the Temple-hall we were too loud;
The garden here is more convenient.

RICHARD

PLANTAGENET

Then say at once if I maintain'd the truth;
Or else was wrangling Somerset in the error?

SUFFOLK

Faith, I have been a truant in the law,
And never yet could frame my will to it;
And therefore frame the law unto my will.

SOMERSET

Judge you, my Lord of Warwick, then, between us.

WARWICK

Between two hawks, which flies the higher pitch;
Between two dogs, which hath the deeper mouth;
Between two blades, which bears the better temper:
Between two horses, which doth bear him best;
Between two girls, which hath the merriest eye;
I have perhaps some shallow spirit of judgement;
But in these nice sharp quillets of the law,
Good faith, I am no wiser than a daw.

RICHARD

PLANTAGENET

Tut, tut, here is a mannerly forbearance:
The truth appears so naked on my side
That any purblind eye may find it out.

SOMERSET

And on my side it is so well apparell'd,
So clear, so shining and so evident
That it will glimmer through a blind man's eye.

RICHARD

PLANTAGENET

Since you are tongue-tied and so loath to speak,
In dumb significants proclaim your thoughts:
Let him that is a true-born gentleman
And stands upon the honour of his birth,
If he suppose that I have pleaded truth,
From off this brier pluck a white rose with me.

SOMERSET

Let him that is no coward nor no flatterer,
But dare maintain the party of the truth,
Pluck a red rose from off this thorn with me.

WARWICK

I love no colours, and without all colour
Of base insinuating flattery
I pluck this white rose with Plantagenet.

SUFFOLK

I pluck this red rose with young Somerset
And say withal I think he held the right.

VERNON

Stay, lords and gentlemen, and pluck no more,
Till you conclude that he upon whose side
The fewest roses are cropp'd from the tree
Shall yield the other in the right opinion.

SOMERSET

Good Master Vernon, it is well objected:
If I have fewest, I subscribe in silence.
RICHARD

PLANTAGENET

And I.

VERNON

Then for the truth and plainness of the case.
I pluck this pale and maiden blossom here,
Giving my verdict on the white rose side.

SOMERSET

Prick not your finger as you pluck it off,
Lest bleeding you do paint the white rose red
And fall on my side so, against your will.

VERNON

If I my lord, for my opinion bleed,
Opinion shall be surgeon to my hurt
And keep me on the side where still I am.

SOMERSET

Well, well, come on: who else?

Lawyer

Unless my study and my books be false,
The argument you held was wrong in you:

To SOMERSET

In sign whereof I pluck a white rose too.
RICHARD

PLANTAGENET

Now, Somerset, where is your argument?

SOMERSET

Here in my scabbard, meditating that
Shall dye your white rose in a bloody red.
RICHARD

PLANTAGENET

Meantime your cheeks do counterfeit our roses;
For pale they look with fear, as witnessing
The truth on our side.

SOMERSET

No, Plantagenet,
'Tis not for fear but anger that thy cheeks
Blush for pure shame to counterfeit our roses,
And yet thy tongue will not confess thy error.
RICHARD

PLANTAGENET

Hath not thy rose a canker, Somerset?

SOMERSET

Hath not thy rose a thorn, Plantagenet?
RICHARD

PLANTAGENET

Ay, sharp and piercing, to maintain his truth;
Whiles thy consuming canker eats his falsehood.

SOMERSET

Well, I'll find friends to wear my bleeding roses,
That shall maintain what I have said is true,
Where false Plantagenet dare not be seen.
RICHARD

PLANTAGENET

Now, by this maiden blossom in my hand,
I scorn thee and thy fashion, peevish boy.

SUFFOLK

Turn not thy scorns this way, Plantagenet.
RICHARD

PLANTAGENET

Proud Pole, I will, and scorn both him and thee.

SUFFOLK

I'll turn my part thereof into thy throat.

SOMERSET

Away, away, good William de la Pole!
We grace the yeoman by conversing with him.

WARWICK

Now, by God's will, thou wrong'st him, Somerset;
His grandfather was Lionel Duke of Clarence,
Third son to the third Edward King of England:
Spring crestless yeomen from so deep a root?
RICHARD

PLANTAGENET

He bears him on the place's privilege,
Or durst not, for his craven heart, say thus.

SOMERSET

By him that made me, I'll maintain my words
On any plot of ground in Christendom.
Was not thy father, Richard Earl of Cambridge,
For treason executed in our late king's days?
And, by his treason, stand'st not thou attainted,
Corrupted, and exempt from ancient gentry?
His trespass yet lives guilty in thy blood;
And, till thou be restored, thou art a yeoman.
RICHARD

PLANTAGENET

My father was attached, not attainted,
Condemn'd to die for treason, but no traitor;
And that I'll prove on better men than Somerset,
Were growing time once ripen'd to my will.
For your partaker Pole and you yourself,
I'll note you in my book of memory,
To scourge you for this apprehension:
Look to it well and say you are well warn'd.

SOMERSET

Ah, thou shalt find us ready for thee still;
And know us by these colours for thy foes,
For these my friends in spite of thee shall wear.
RICHARD

PLANTAGENET

And, by my soul, this pale and angry rose,
As cognizance of my blood-drinking hate,
Will I for ever and my faction wear,
Until it wither with me to my grave
Or flourish to the height of my degree.

SUFFOLK

Go forward and be choked with thy ambition!
And so farewell until I meet thee next.

Exit

SOMERSET

Have with thee, Pole. Farewell, ambitious Richard.

Exit

RICHARD

PLANTAGENET

How I am braved and must perforce endure it!

WARWICK

This blot that they object against your house
Shall be wiped out in the next parliament
Call'd for the truce of Winchester and Gloucester;
And if thou be not then created York,
I will not live to be accounted Warwick.
Meantime, in signal of my love to thee,
Against proud Somerset and William Pole,
Will I upon thy party wear this rose:
And here I prophesy: this brawl to-day,
Grown to this faction in the Temple-garden,
Shall send between the red rose and the white
A thousand souls to death and deadly night.
RICHARD

PLANTAGENET

Good Master Vernon, I am bound to you,
That you on my behalf would pluck a flower.

VERNON

In your behalf still will I wear the same.

Lawyer

And so will I.
RICHARD

PLANTAGENET

Thanks, gentle sir.
Come, let us four to dinner: I dare say
This quarrel will drink blood another day.

Exeunt

SCENE V. The Tower of London.

Enter MORTIMER, brought in a chair, and Gaolers

MORTIMER

Kind keepers of my weak decaying age,
Let dying Mortimer here rest himself.
Even like a man new haled from the rack,
So fare my limbs with long imprisonment.
And these grey locks, the pursuivants of death,
Nestor-like aged in an age of care,
Argue the end of Edmund Mortimer.
These eyes, like lamps whose wasting oil is spent,
Wax dim, as drawing to their exigent;
Weak shoulders, overborne with burthening grief,
And pithless arms, like to a wither'd vine
That droops his sapless branches to the ground;
Yet are these feet, whose strengthless stay is numb,
Unable to support this lump of clay,
Swift-winged with desire to get a grave,
As witting I no other comfort have.
But tell me, keeper, will my nephew come?

First Gaoler

Richard Plantagenet, my lord, will come:
We sent unto the Temple, unto his chamber;
And answer was return'd that he will come.

MORTIMER

Enough: my soul shall then be satisfied.
Poor gentleman! his wrong doth equal mine.
Since Henry Monmouth first began to reign,
Before whose glory I was great in arms,

This loathsome sequestration have I had:
And even since then hath Richard been obscured,
Deprived of honour and inheritance.
But now the arbitrator of despairs,
Just death, kind umpire of men's miseries,
With sweet enlargement doth dismiss me hence:
I would his troubles likewise were expired,
That so he might recover what was lost.

Enter RICHARD PLANTAGENET

First Gaoler

My lord, your loving nephew now is come.

MORTIMER

Richard Plantagenet, my friend, is he come?
RICHARD

PLANTAGENET

Ay, noble uncle, thus ignobly used,
Your nephew, late despised Richard, comes.

MORTIMER

Direct mine arms I may embrace his neck,
And in his bosom spend my latter gasp:
O, tell me when my lips do touch his cheeks,
That I may kindly give one fainting kiss.
And now declare, sweet stem from York's great stock,
Why didst thou say, of late thou wert despised?
RICHARD

PLANTAGENET

First, lean thine aged back against mine arm;
And, in that ease, I'll tell thee my disease.
This day, in argument upon a case,
Some words there grew 'twixt Somerset and me;
Among which terms he used his lavish tongue
And did upbraid me with my father's death:
Which obloquy set bars before my tongue,
Else with the like I had requited him.

Therefore, good uncle, for my father's sake,
In honour of a true Plantagenet
And for alliance sake, declare the cause
My father, Earl of Cambridge, lost his head.

MORTIMER

That cause, fair nephew, that imprison'd me
And hath detain'd me all my flowering youth
Within a loathsome dungeon, there to pine,
Was cursed instrument of his decease.

RICHARD

PLANTAGENET

Discover more at large what cause that was,
For I am ignorant and cannot guess.

MORTIMER

I will, if that my fading breath permit
And death approach not ere my tale be done.
Henry the Fourth, grandfather to this king,
Deposed his nephew Richard, Edward's son,
The first-begotten and the lawful heir,
Of Edward king, the third of that descent:
During whose reign the Percies of the north,
Finding his usurpation most unjust,
Endeavor'd my advancement to the throne:
The reason moved these warlike lords to this
Was, for that--young King Richard thus removed,
Leaving no heir begotten of his body--
I was the next by birth and parentage;
For by my mother I derived am
From Lionel Duke of Clarence, the third son
To King Edward the Third; whereas he
From John of Gaunt doth bring his pedigree,
Being but fourth of that heroic line.
But mark: as in this haughty attempt
They laboured to plant the rightful heir,
I lost my liberty and they their lives.
Long after this, when Henry the Fifth,

Succeeding his father Bolingbroke, did reign,
Thy father, Earl of Cambridge, then derived
From famous Edmund Langley, Duke of York,
Marrying my sister that thy mother was,
Again in pity of my hard distress
Levied an army, weening to redeem
And have install'd me in the diadem:
But, as the rest, so fell that noble earl
And was beheaded. Thus the Mortimers,
In whom the tide rested, were suppress'd.
RICHARD

PLANTAGENET

Of which, my lord, your honour is the last.

MORTIMER

True; and thou seest that I no issue have
And that my fainting words do warrant death;
Thou art my heir; the rest I wish thee gather:
But yet be wary in thy studious care.
RICHARD

PLANTAGENET

Thy grave admonishments prevail with me:
But yet, methinks, my father's execution
Was nothing less than bloody tyranny.

MORTIMER

With silence, nephew, be thou politic:
Strong-fixed is the house of Lancaster,
And like a mountain, not to be removed.
But now thy uncle is removing hence:
As princes do their courts, when they are cloy'd
With long continuance in a settled place.
RICHARD

PLANTAGENET

O, uncle, would some part of my young years
Might but redeem the passage of your age!

MORTIMER

Thou dost then wrong me, as that slaughterer doth
Which giveth many wounds when one will kill.
Mourn not, except thou sorrow for my good;
Only give order for my funeral:
And so farewell, and fair be all thy hopes
And prosperous be thy life in peace and war!

Dies

RICHARD

PLANTAGENET

And peace, no war, befall thy parting soul!
In prison hast thou spent a pilgrimage
And like a hermit overpass'd thy days.
Well, I will lock his counsel in my breast;
And what I do imagine let that rest.
Keepers, convey him hence, and I myself
Will see his burial better than his life.

Exeunt Gaolers, bearing out the body of MORTIMER

Here dies the dusky torch of Mortimer,
Choked with ambition of the meaner sort:
And for those wrongs, those bitter injuries,
Which Somerset hath offer'd to my house:
I doubt not but with honour to redress;
And therefore haste I to the parliament,
Either to be restored to my blood,
Or make my ill the advantage of my good.

Exit

ACT III

SCENE I. London. The Parliament-house.

Flourish. Enter KING HENRY VI, EXETER, GLOUCESTER, WARWICK, SOMERSET, and SUFFOLK; the BISHOP OF WINCHESTER, RICHARD PLANTAGENET, and others. GLOUCESTER offers to put up a bill; BISHOP OF WINCHESTER snatches it, and tears it

BISHOP

OF WINCHESTER

Comest thou with deep premeditated lines,
With written pamphlets studiously devised,
Humphrey of Gloucester? If thou canst accuse,
Or aught intend'st to lay unto my charge,
Do it without invention, suddenly;
As I with sudden and extemporal speech
Purpose to answer what thou canst object.

GLOUCESTER

Presumptuous priest! this place commands my patience,
Or thou shouldst find thou hast dishonour'd me.
Think not, although in writing I preferr'd
The manner of thy vile outrageous crimes,
That therefore I have forged, or am not able
Verbatim to rehearse the method of my pen:
No, prelate; such is thy audacious wickedness,
Thy lewd, pestiferous and dissentious pranks,
As very infants prattle of thy pride.

Thou art a most pernicious usurer,
Forward by nature, enemy to peace;
Lascivious, wanton, more than well beseems
A man of thy profession and degree;
And for thy treachery, what's more manifest?
In that thou laid'st a trap to take my life,
As well at London bridge as at the Tower.
Beside, I fear me, if thy thoughts were sifted,
The king, thy sovereign, is not quite exempt
From envious malice of thy swelling heart.
BISHOP

OF WINCHESTER

Gloucester, I do defy thee. Lords, vouchsafe
To give me hearing what I shall reply.
If I were covetous, ambitious or perverse,
As he will have me, how am I so poor?
Or how haps it I seek not to advance
Or raise myself, but keep my wonted calling?
And for dissension, who preferreth peace
More than I do?--except I be provoked.
No, my good lords, it is not that offends;
It is not that that hath incensed the duke:
It is, because no one should sway but he;
No one but he should be about the king;
And that engenders thunder in his breast
And makes him roar these accusations forth.
But he shall know I am as good--

GLOUCESTER

As good!
Thou bastard of my grandfather!
BISHOP

OF WINCHESTER

Ay, lordly sir; for what are you, I pray,
But one imperious in another's throne?

GLOUCESTER

Am I not protector, saucy priest?

BISHOP

OF WINCHESTER

And am not I a prelate of the church?

GLOUCESTER

Yes, as an outlaw in a castle keeps
And useth it to patronage his theft.

BISHOP

OF WINCHESTER

Unreverent Gloster!

GLOUCESTER

Thou art reverent
Touching thy spiritual function, not thy life.

BISHOP

OF WINCHESTER

Rome shall remedy this.

WARWICK

Roam thither, then.

SOMERSET

My lord, it were your duty to forbear.

WARWICK

Ay, see the bishop be not overborne.

SOMERSET

Methinks my lord should be religious
And know the office that belongs to such.

WARWICK

Methinks his lordship should be humbler;
it fitteth not a prelate so to plead.

SOMERSET

Yes, when his holy state is touch'd so near.

WARWICK

State holy or unhallow'd, what of that?
Is not his grace protector to the king?

RICHARD

PLANTAGENET

[Aside] Plantagenet, I see, must hold his tongue,
Lest it be said 'Speak, sirrah, when you should;
Must your bold verdict enter talk with lords?'
Else would I have a fling at Winchester.

KING HENRY VI

Uncles of Gloucester and of Winchester,
The special watchmen of our English weal,
I would prevail, if prayers might prevail,
To join your hearts in love and amity.
O, what a scandal is it to our crown,
That two such noble peers as ye should jar!
Believe me, lords, my tender years can tell
Civil dissension is a viperous worm
That gnaws the bowels of the commonwealth.

A noise within, 'Down with the tawny-coats!'

What tumult's this?

WARWICK

An uproar, I dare warrant,
Begun through malice of the bishop's men.

A noise again, 'Stones! stones!' Enter Mayor

Mayor

O, my good lords, and virtuous Henry,
Pity the city of London, pity us!
The bishop and the Duke of Gloucester's men,
Forbidden late to carry any weapon,
Have fill'd their pockets full of pebble stones
And banding themselves in contrary parts
Do pelt so fast at one another's pate
That many have their giddy brains knock'd out:

Our windows are broke down in every street
And we for fear compell'd to shut our shops.

Enter Serving-men, in skirmish, with bloody pates

KING HENRY VI

We charge you, on allegiance to ourself,
To hold your slaughtering hands and keep the peace.
Pray, uncle Gloucester, mitigate this strife.
First Serving-man Nay, if we be forbidden stones,
We'll fall to it with our teeth.
Second Serving-man Do what ye dare, we are as resolute.

Skirmish again

GLOUCESTER

You of my household, leave this peevish broil
And set this unaccustom'd fight aside.
Third Serving-man My lord, we know your grace to be a man
Just and upright; and, for your royal birth,
Inferior to none but to his majesty:
And ere that we will suffer such a prince,
So kind a father of the commonweal,
To be disgraced by an inkhorn mate,
We and our wives and children all will fight
And have our bodies slaughtered by thy foes.
First Serving-man Ay, and the very parings of our nails
Shall pitch a field when we are dead.

Begin again

GLOUCESTER

Stay, stay, I say!
And if you love me, as you say you do,
Let me persuade you to forbear awhile.

KING HENRY VI

O, how this discord doth afflict my soul!
Can you, my Lord of Winchester, behold
My sighs and tears and will not once relent?
Who should be pitiful, if you be not?

Or who should study to prefer a peace.
If holy churchmen take delight in broils?

WARWICK

Yield, my lord protector; yield, Winchester;
Except you mean with obstinate repulse
To slay your sovereign and destroy the realm.
You see what mischief and what murder too
Hath been enacted through your enmity;
Then be at peace except ye thirst for blood.
BISHOP

OF WINCHESTER

He shall submit, or I will never yield.

GLOUCESTER

Compassion on the king commands me stoop;
Or I would see his heart out, ere the priest
Should ever get that privilege of me.

WARWICK

Behold, my Lord of Winchester, the duke
Hath banish'd moody discontented fury,
As by his smoothed brows it doth appear:
Why look you still so stern and tragical?

GLOUCESTER

Here, Winchester, I offer thee my hand.

KING HENRY VI

Fie, uncle Beaufort! I have heard you preach
That malice was a great and grievous sin;
And will not you maintain the thing you teach,
But prove a chief offender in the same?

WARWICK

Sweet king! the bishop hath a kindly gird.
For shame, my lord of Winchester, relent!
What, shall a child instruct you what to do?
BISHOP

OF WINCHESTER

Well, Duke of Gloucester, I will yield to thee;
Love for thy love and hand for hand I give.

GLOUCESTER

[Aside] Ay, but, I fear me, with a hollow heart.--
See here, my friends and loving countrymen,
This token serveth for a flag of truce
Betwixt ourselves and all our followers:
So help me God, as I dissemble not!
BISHOP

OF WINCHESTER

[Aside] So help me God, as I intend it not!

KING HENRY VI

O, loving uncle, kind Duke of Gloucester,
How joyful am I made by this contract!
Away, my masters! trouble us no more;
But join in friendship, as your lords have done.
First Serving-man Content: I'll to the surgeon's.
Second Serving-man And so will I.
Third Serving-man And I will see what physic the tavern affords.

Exeunt Serving-men, Mayor, & c

WARWICK

Accept this scroll, most gracious sovereign,
Which in the right of Richard Plantagenet
We do exhibit to your majesty.

GLOUCESTER

Well urged, my Lord of Warwick: or sweet prince,
And if your grace mark every circumstance,
You have great reason to do Richard right;
Especially for those occasions
At Eltham Place I told your majesty.

KING HENRY VI

And those occasions, uncle, were of force:
Therefore, my loving lords, our pleasure is
That Richard be restored to his blood.

WARWICK

Let Richard be restored to his blood;
So shall his father's wrongs be recompensed.
BISHOP

OF WINCHESTER

As will the rest, so willeth Winchester.

KING HENRY VI

If Richard will be true, not that alone
But all the whole inheritance I give
That doth belong unto the house of York,
From whence you spring by lineal descent.
RICHARD

PLANTAGENET

Thy humble servant vows obedience
And humble service till the point of death.

KING HENRY VI

Stoop then and set your knee against my foot;
And, in reguerdon of that duty done,
I gird thee with the valiant sword of York:
Rise Richard, like a true Plantagenet,
And rise created princely Duke of York.
RICHARD

PLANTAGENET

And so thrive Richard as thy foes may fall!
And as my duty springs, so perish they
That grudge one thought against your majesty!

ALL

Welcome, high prince, the mighty Duke of York!

SOMERSET

[Aside] Perish, base prince, ignoble Duke of York!

GLOUCESTER

Now will it best avail your majesty
To cross the seas and to be crown'd in France:
The presence of a king engenders love
Amongst his subjects and his loyal friends,
As it disanimates his enemies.

KING HENRY VI

When Gloucester says the word, King Henry goes;
For friendly counsel cuts off many foes.

GLOUCESTER

Your ships already are in readiness.

Sennet. Flourish. Exeunt all but EXETER

EXETER

Ay, we may march in England or in France,
Not seeing what is likely to ensue.
This late dissension grown betwixt the peers
Burns under feigned ashes of forged love
And will at last break out into a flame:
As fester'd members rot but by degree,
Till bones and flesh and sinews fall away,
So will this base and envious discord breed.
And now I fear that fatal prophecy
Which in the time of Henry named the Fifth
Was in the mouth of every sucking babe;
That Henry born at Monmouth should win all
And Henry born at Windsor lose all:
Which is so plain that Exeter doth wish
His days may finish ere that hapless time.

Exit

SCENE II. France. Before Rouen.

Enter JOAN LA PUCELLE disguised, with four Soldiers with sacks upon their backs

JOAN LA PUCELLE

These are the city gates, the gates of Rouen,
Through which our policy must make a breach:
Take heed, be wary how you place your words;
Talk like the vulgar sort of market men
That come to gather money for their corn.
If we have entrance, as I hope we shall,
And that we find the slothful watch but weak,
I'll by a sign give notice to our friends,
That Charles the Dauphin may encounter them.

First Soldier

Our sacks shall be a mean to sack the city,
And we be lords and rulers over Rouen;
Therefore we'll knock.

Knocks

Watch

[Within] Qui est la?

JOAN LA PUCELLE

Paysans, pauvres gens de France;
Poor market folks that come to sell their corn.

Watch

Enter, go in; the market bell is rung.

JOAN LA PUCELLE

Now, Rouen, I'll shake thy bulwarks to the ground.

Exeunt

Enter CHARLES, the BASTARD OF ORLEANS, ALENCON, REIGNIER, and forces

CHARLES

Saint Denis bless this happy stratagem!
And once again we'll sleep secure in Rouen.

BASTARD OF ORLEANS

Here enter'd Pucelle and her practisants;
Now she is there, how will she specify
Where is the best and safest passage in?

REIGNIER

By thrusting out a torch from yonder tower;
Which, once discern'd, shows that her meaning is,
No way to that, for weakness, which she enter'd.

Enter JOAN LA PUCELLE on the top, thrusting out a torch burning

JOAN LA PUCELLE

Behold, this is the happy wedding torch
That joineth Rouen unto her countrymen,
But burning fatal to the Talbotites!

Exit

BASTARD OF ORLEANS

See, noble Charles, the beacon of our friend;
The burning torch in yonder turret stands.

CHARLES

Now shine it like a comet of revenge,
A prophet to the fall of all our foes!

REIGNIER

Defer no time, delays have dangerous ends;
Enter, and cry 'The Dauphin!' presently,
And then do execution on the watch.

Alarum. Exeunt

An alarum. Enter TALBOT in an excursion

TALBOT

France, thou shalt rue this treason with thy tears,
If Talbot but survive thy treachery.
Pucelle, that witch, that damned sorceress,
Hath wrought this hellish mischief unawares,
That hardly we escaped the pride of France.

Exit

An alarum: excursions. BEDFORD, brought in sick in a chair. Enter
TALBOT and BURGUNDY without: within JOAN LA PUCELLE,
CHARLES, BASTARD OF ORLEANS, ALENCON, and REIGNIER, on the
walls

JOAN LA PUCELLE

Good morrow, gallants! want ye corn for bread?
I think the Duke of Burgundy will fast
Before he'll buy again at such a rate:
'Twas full of darnel; do you like the taste?

BURGUNDY

Scoff on, vile fiend and shameless courtezan!
I trust ere long to choke thee with thine own
And make thee curse the harvest of that corn.

CHARLES

Your grace may starve perhaps before that time.

BEDFORD

O, let no words, but deeds, revenge this treason!

JOAN LA PUCELLE

What will you do, good grey-beard? break a lance,
And run a tilt at death within a chair?

TALBOT

Foul fiend of France, and hag of all despite,
Encompass'd with thy lustful paramours!
Becomes it thee to taunt his valiant age
And twit with cowardice a man half dead?
Damsel, I'll have a bout with you again,
Or else let Talbot perish with this shame.

JOAN LA PUCELLE

Are ye so hot, sir? yet, Pucelle, hold thy peace;
If Talbot do but thunder, rain will follow.

The English whisper together in council

God speed the parliament! who shall be the speaker?

TALBOT

Dare ye come forth and meet us in the field?

JOAN LA PUCELLE

Belike your lordship takes us then for fools,
To try if that our own be ours or no.

TALBOT

I speak not to that railing Hecate,
But unto thee, Alencon, and the rest;
Will ye, like soldiers, come and fight it out?

ALENCON

Signior, no.

TALBOT

Signior, hang! base muleters of France!
Like peasant foot-boys do they keep the walls
And dare not take up arms like gentlemen.

JOAN LA PUCELLE

Away, captains! let's get us from the walls;
For Talbot means no goodness by his looks.
God be wi' you, my lord! we came but to tell you
That we are here.

Exeunt from the walls

TALBOT

And there will we be too, ere it be long,
Or else reproach be Talbot's greatest fame!
Vow, Burgundy, by honour of thy house,
Prick'd on by public wrongs sustain'd in France,
Either to get the town again or die:
And I, as sure as English Henry lives
And as his father here was conqueror,
As sure as in this late-betrayed town
Great Coeur-de-lion's heart was buried,
So sure I swear to get the town or die.

BURGUNDY

My vows are equal partners with thy vows.

TALBOT

But, ere we go, regard this dying prince,
The valiant Duke of Bedford. Come, my lord,
We will bestow you in some better place,
Fitter for sickness and for crazy age.

BEDFORD

Lord Talbot, do not so dishonour me:
Here will I sit before the walls of Rouen
And will be partner of your weal or woe.

BURGUNDY

Courageous Bedford, let us now persuade you.

BEDFORD

Not to be gone from hence; for once I read
That stout Pendragon in his litter sick
Came to the field and vanquished his foes:
Methinks I should revive the soldiers' hearts,
Because I ever found them as myself.

TALBOT

Undaunted spirit in a dying breast!
Then be it so: heavens keep old Bedford safe!
And now no more ado, brave Burgundy,
But gather we our forces out of hand
And set upon our boasting enemy.

Exeunt all but BEDFORD and Attendants

An alarum: excursions. Enter FASTOLFE and a Captain

Captain

Whither away, Sir John Fastolfe, in such haste?

FASTOLFE

Whither away! to save myself by flight:
We are like to have the overthrow again.

Captain

What! will you fly, and leave Lord Talbot?

FASTOLFE

Ay,
All the Talbots in the world, to save my life!

Exit

Captain

Cowardly knight! ill fortune follow thee!

Exit

Retreat: excursions. JOAN LA PUCELLE, ALENCON, and CHARLES fly

BEDFORD

Now, quiet soul, depart when heaven please,
For I have seen our enemies' overthrow.
What is the trust or strength of foolish man?
They that of late were daring with their scoffs
Are glad and fain by flight to save themselves.

BEDFORD dies, and is carried in by two in his chair

An alarum. Re-enter TALBOT, BURGUNDY, and the rest

TALBOT

Lost, and recover'd in a day again!
This is a double honour, Burgundy:
Yet heavens have glory for this victory!

BURGUNDY

Warlike and martial Talbot, Burgundy
Enshrines thee in his heart and there erects
Thy noble deeds as valour's monuments.

TALBOT

Thanks, gentle duke. But where is Pucelle now?
I think her old familiar is asleep:
Now where's the Bastard's braves, and Charles his gleeks?
What, all amort? Rouen hangs her head for grief
That such a valiant company are fled.

Now will we take some order in the town,
Placing therein some expert officers,
And then depart to Paris to the king,
For there young Henry with his nobles lie.

BURGUNDY

What wills Lord Talbot pleaseth Burgundy.

TALBOT

But yet, before we go, let's not forget
The noble Duke of Bedford late deceased,
But see his exequies fulfill'd in Rouen:
A braver soldier never couched lance,
A gentler heart did never sway in court;
But kings and mightiest potentates must die,
For that's the end of human misery.

Exeunt

SCENE III. The plains near Rouen.

Enter CHARLES, the BASTARD OF ORLEANS, ALENCON, JOAN LA PUCELLE, and forces

JOAN LA PUCELLE

Dismay not, princes, at this accident,
Nor grieve that Rouen is so recovered:
Care is no cure, but rather corrosive,
For things that are not to be remedied.
Let frantic Talbot triumph for a while
And like a peacock sweep along his tail;
We'll pull his plumes and take away his train,
If Dauphin and the rest will be but ruled.

CHARLES

We have been guided by thee hitherto,
And of thy cunning had no diffidence:
One sudden foil shall never breed distrust.

BASTARD OF ORLEANS

Search out thy wit for secret policies,
And we will make thee famous through the world.

ALENCON

We'll set thy statue in some holy place,
And have thee reverenced like a blessed saint:
Employ thee then, sweet virgin, for our good.

JOAN LA PUCELLE

Then thus it must be; this doth Joan devise:
By fair persuasions mix'd with sugar'd words
We will entice the Duke of Burgundy
To leave the Talbot and to follow us.

CHARLES

Ay, marry, sweeting, if we could do that,
France were no place for Henry's warriors;
Nor should that nation boast it so with us,
But be extirped from our provinces.

ALENCON

For ever should they be expulsed from France
And not have title of an earldom here.

JOAN LA PUCELLE

Your honours shall perceive how I will work
To bring this matter to the wished end.

Drum sounds afar off

Hark! by the sound of drum you may perceive
Their powers are marching unto Paris-ward.

Here sound an English march. Enter, and pass over at a distance,
TALBOT and his forces

There goes the Talbot, with his colours spread,
And all the troops of English after him.

French march. Enter BURGUNDY and forces

Now in the rearward comes the duke and his:
Fortune in favour makes him lag behind.
Summon a parley; we will talk with him.

Trumpets sound a parley

CHARLES

A parley with the Duke of Burgundy!

BURGUNDY

Who craves a parley with the Burgundy?

JOAN LA PUCELLE

The princely Charles of France, thy countryman.

BURGUNDY

What say'st thou, Charles? for I am marching hence.

CHARLES

Speak, Pucelle, and enchant him with thy words.

JOAN LA PUCELLE

Brave Burgundy, undoubted hope of France!
Stay, let thy humble handmaid speak to thee.

BURGUNDY

Speak on; but be not over-tedious.

JOAN LA PUCELLE

Look on thy country, look on fertile France,
And see the cities and the towns defaced
By wasting ruin of the cruel foe.
As looks the mother on her lowly babe
When death doth close his tender dying eyes,
See, see the pining malady of France;
Behold the wounds, the most unnatural wounds,
Which thou thyself hast given her woful breast.
O, turn thy edged sword another way;
Strike those that hurt, and hurt not those that help.
One drop of blood drawn from thy country's bosom
Should grieve thee more than streams of foreign gore:
Return thee therefore with a flood of tears,
And wash away thy country's stained spots.

BURGUNDY

Either she hath bewitch'd me with her words,
Or nature makes me suddenly relent.

JOAN LA PUCELLE

Besides, all French and France exclaims on thee,
Doubting thy birth and lawful progeny.
Who joint'st thou with but with a lordly nation
That will not trust thee but for profit's sake?
When Talbot hath set footing once in France
And fashion'd thee that instrument of ill,
Who then but English Henry will be lord
And thou be thrust out like a fugitive?
Call we to mind, and mark but this for proof,
Was not the Duke of Orleans thy foe?
And was he not in England prisoner?
But when they heard he was thine enemy,
They set him free without his ransom paid,
In spite of Burgundy and all his friends.
See, then, thou fight'st against thy countrymen
And joint'st with them will be thy slaughtermen.
Come, come, return; return, thou wandering lord:
Charles and the rest will take thee in their arms.

BURGUNDY

I am vanquished; these haughty words of hers
Have batter'd me like roaring cannon-shot,
And made me almost yield upon my knees.
Forgive me, country, and sweet countrymen,
And, lords, accept this hearty kind embrace:
My forces and my power of men are yours:
So farewell, Talbot; I'll no longer trust thee.

JOAN LA PUCELLE

[Aside] Done like a Frenchman: turn, and turn again!

CHARLES

Welcome, brave duke! thy friendship makes us fresh.

BASTARD OF ORLEANS

And doth beget new courage in our breasts.

ALENCON

Pucelle hath bravely play'd her part in this,
And doth deserve a coronet of gold.

CHARLES

Now let us on, my lords, and join our powers,
And seek how we may prejudice the foe.

Exeunt

SCENE IV. Paris. The palace.

*Enter KING HENRY VI, GLOUCESTER, BISHOP OF WINCHESTER,
YORK, SUFFOLK, SOMERSET, WARWICK, EXETER, VERNON BASSET,
and others. To them with his Soldiers, TALBOT*

TALBOT

My gracious prince, and honourable peers,
Hearing of your arrival in this realm,
I have awhile given truce unto my wars,
To do my duty to my sovereign:
In sign, whereof, this arm, that hath reclaim'd
To your obedience fifty fortresses,
Twelve cities and seven walled towns of strength,
Beside five hundred prisoners of esteem,
Lets fall his sword before your highness' feet,
And with submissive loyalty of heart
Ascribes the glory of his conquest got
First to my God and next unto your grace.

Kneels

KING HENRY VI

Is this the Lord Talbot, uncle Gloucester,
That hath so long been resident in France?

GLOUCESTER

Yes, if it please your majesty, my liege.

KING HENRY VI

Welcome, brave captain and victorious lord!
When I was young, as yet I am not old,
I do remember how my father said
A stouter champion never handled sword.
Long since we were resolved of your truth,
Your faithful service and your toil in war;

Yet never have you tasted our reward,
Or been reguerdon'd with so much as thanks,
Because till now we never saw your face:
Therefore, stand up; and, for these good deserts,
We here create you Earl of Shrewsbury;
And in our coronation take your place.

Sennet. Flourish. Exeunt all but VERNON and BASSET

VERNON

Now, sir, to you, that were so hot at sea,
Disgracing of these colours that I wear
In honour of my noble Lord of York:
Darest thou maintain the former words thou spakest?

BASSET

Yes, sir; as well as you dare patronage
The envious barking of your saucy tongue
Against my lord the Duke of Somerset.

VERNON

Sirrah, thy lord I honour as he is.

BASSET

Why, what is he? as good a man as York.

VERNON

Hark ye; not so: in witness, take ye that.

Strikes him

BASSET

Villain, thou know'st the law of arms is such
That whoso draws a sword, 'tis present death,
Or else this blow should broach thy dearest blood.
But I'll unto his majesty, and crave
I may have liberty to venge this wrong;
When thou shalt see I'll meet thee to thy cost.

VERNON

Well, miscreant, I'll be there as soon as you;
And, after, meet you sooner than you would.

Exeunt

ACT IV

SCENE I. Paris. A hall of state.

Enter KING HENRY VI, GLOUCESTER, BISHOP OF WINCHESTER, YORK, SUFFOLK, SOMERSET, WARWICK, TALBOT, EXETER, the Governor, of Paris, and others

GLOUCESTER

Lord bishop, set the crown upon his head.
BISHOP

OF WINCHESTER

God save King Henry, of that name the sixth!

GLOUCESTER

Now, governor of Paris, take your oath,
That you elect no other king but him;
Esteem none friends but such as are his friends,
And none your foes but such as shall pretend
Malicious practises against his state:
This shall ye do, so help you righteous God!

Enter FASTOLFE

FASTOLFE

My gracious sovereign, as I rode from Calais,
To haste unto your coronation,
A letter was deliver'd to my hands,
Writ to your grace from the Duke of Burgundy.

TALBOT

Shame to the Duke of Burgundy and thee!
I vow'd, base knight, when I did meet thee next,
To tear the garter from thy craven's leg,

Plucking it off
Which I have done, because unworthily
Thou wast installed in that high degree.
Pardon me, princely Henry, and the rest
This dastard, at the battle of Patay,
When but in all I was six thousand strong
And that the French were almost ten to one,
Before we met or that a stroke was given,
Like to a trusty squire did run away:
In which assault we lost twelve hundred men;
Myself and divers gentlemen beside
Were there surprised and taken prisoners.
Then judge, great lords, if I have done amiss;
Or whether that such cowards ought to wear
This ornament of knighthood, yea or no.

GLOUCESTER

To say the truth, this fact was infamous
And ill beseeming any common man,
Much more a knight, a captain and a leader.

TALBOT

When first this order was ordain'd, my lords,
Knights of the garter were of noble birth,
Valiant and virtuous, full of haughty courage,
Such as were grown to credit by the wars;
Not fearing death, nor shrinking for distress,
But always resolute in most extremes.
He then that is not furnish'd in this sort
Doth but usurp the sacred name of knight,
Profaning this most honourable order,
And should, if I were worthy to be judge,
Be quite degraded, like a hedge-born swain
That doth presume to boast of gentle blood.

KING HENRY VI

Stain to thy countrymen, thou hear'st thy doom!
Be packing, therefore, thou that wast a knight:
Henceforth we banish thee, on pain of death.

Exit FASTOLFE

And now, my lord protector, view the letter
Sent from our uncle Duke of Burgundy.

GLOUCESTER

What means his grace, that he hath changed his style?
No more but, plain and bluntly, 'To the king!'
Hath he forgot he is his sovereign?
Or doth this churlish superscription
Pretend some alteration in good will?
What's here?

Reads

'I have, upon especial cause,
Moved with compassion of my country's wreck,
Together with the pitiful complaints
Of such as your oppression feeds upon,
Forsaken your pernicious faction
And join'd with Charles, the rightful King of France.'
O monstrous treachery! can this be so,
That in alliance, amity and oaths,
There should be found such false dissembling guile?

KING HENRY VI

What! doth my uncle Burgundy revolt?

GLOUCESTER

He doth, my lord, and is become your foe.

KING HENRY VI

Is that the worst this letter doth contain?

GLOUCESTER

It is the worst, and all, my lord, he writes.

KING HENRY VI

Why, then, Lord Talbot there shall talk with him
And give him chastisement for this abuse.
How say you, my lord? are you not content?

TALBOT

Content, my liege! yes, but that I am prevented,
I should have begg'd I might have been employ'd.

KING HENRY VI

Then gather strength and march unto him straight:
Let him perceive how ill we brook his treason
And what offence it is to flout his friends.

TALBOT

I go, my lord, in heart desiring still
You may behold confusion of your foes.

Exit

Enter VERNON and BASSET

VERNON

Grant me the combat, gracious sovereign.

BASSET

And me, my lord, grant me the combat too.

YORK

This is my servant: hear him, noble prince.

SOMERSET

And this is mine: sweet Henry, favour him.

KING HENRY VI

Be patient, lords; and give them leave to speak.
Say, gentlemen, what makes you thus exclaim?
And wherefore crave you combat? or with whom?

VERNON

With him, my lord; for he hath done me wrong.

BASSET

And I with him; for he hath done me wrong.

KING HENRY VI

What is that wrong whereof you both complain?
First let me know, and then I'll answer you.

BASSET

Crossing the sea from England into France,
This fellow here, with envious carping tongue,
Upbraided me about the rose I wear;
Saying, the sanguine colour of the leaves
Did represent my master's blushing cheeks,
When stubbornly he did repugn the truth
About a certain question in the law
Argued betwixt the Duke of York and him;
With other vile and ignominious terms:
In confutation of which rude reproach
And in defence of my lord's worthiness,
I crave the benefit of law of arms.

VERNON

And that is my petition, noble lord:
For though he seem with forged quaint conceit
To set a gloss upon his bold intent,
Yet know, my lord, I was provoked by him;
And he first took exceptions at this badge,
Pronouncing that the paleness of this flower
Bewray'd the faintness of my master's heart.

YORK

Will not this malice, Somerset, be left?

SOMERSET

Your private grudge, my Lord of York, will out,
Though ne'er so cunningly you smother it.

KING HENRY VI

Good Lord, what madness rules in brainsick men,
When for so slight and frivolous a cause

Such factious emulations shall arise!
Good cousins both, of York and Somerset,
Quiet yourselves, I pray, and be at peace.

YORK

Let this dissension first be tried by fight,
And then your highness shall command a peace.

SOMERSET

The quarrel toucheth none but us alone;
Betwixt ourselves let us decide it then.

YORK

There is my pledge; accept it, Somerset.

VERNON

Nay, let it rest where it began at first.

BASSET

Confirm it so, mine honourable lord.

GLOUCESTER

Confirm it so! Confounded be your strife!
And perish ye, with your audacious prate!
Presumptuous vassals, are you not ashamed
With this immodest clamorous outrage
To trouble and disturb the king and us?
And you, my lords, methinks you do not well
To bear with their perverse objections;
Much less to take occasion from their mouths
To raise a mutiny betwixt yourselves:
Let me persuade you take a better course.

EXETER

It grieves his highness: good my lords, be friends.

KING HENRY VI

Come hither, you that would be combatants:
Henceforth I charge you, as you love our favour,
Quite to forget this quarrel and the cause.
And you, my lords, remember where we are,

In France, amongst a fickle wavering nation:
If they perceive dissension in our looks
And that within ourselves we disagree,
How will their grudging stomachs be provoked
To wilful disobedience, and rebel!
Beside, what infamy will there arise,
When foreign princes shall be certified
That for a toy, a thing of no regard,
King Henry's peers and chief nobility
Destroy'd themselves, and lost the realm of France!
O, think upon the conquest of my father,
My tender years, and let us not forego
That for a trifle that was bought with blood
Let me be umpire in this doubtful strife.
I see no reason, if I wear this rose,

Putting on a red rose

That any one should therefore be suspicious
I more incline to Somerset than York:
Both are my kinsmen, and I love them both:
As well they may upbraid me with my crown,
Because, forsooth, the king of Scots is crown'd.
But your discretions better can persuade
Than I am able to instruct or teach:
And therefore, as we hither came in peace,
So let us still continue peace and love.
Cousin of York, we institute your grace
To be our regent in these parts of France:
And, good my Lord of Somerset, unite
Your troops of horsemen with his bands of foot;
And, like true subjects, sons of your progenitors,
Go cheerfully together and digest.
Your angry choler on your enemies.
Ourself, my lord protector and the rest
After some respite will return to Calais;
From thence to England; where I hope ere long
To be presented, by your victories,
With Charles, Alencon and that traitorous rout.

Flourish. Exeunt all but YORK, WARWICK, EXETER and VERNON

WARWICK

My Lord of York, I promise you, the king
Prettily, methought, did play the orator.

YORK

And so he did; but yet I like it not,
In that he wears the badge of Somerset.

WARWICK

Tush, that was but his fancy, blame him not;
I dare presume, sweet prince, he thought no harm.

YORK

An if I wist he did,--but let it rest;
Other affairs must now be managed.

Exeunt all but EXETER

EXETER

Well didst thou, Richard, to suppress thy voice;
For, had the passions of thy heart burst out,
I fear we should have seen decipher'd there
More rancorous spite, more furious raging broils,
Than yet can be imagined or supposed.
But howsoe'er, no simple man that sees
This jarring discord of nobility,
This shouldering of each other in the court,
This factious bandying of their favourites,
But that it doth presage some ill event.
'Tis much when sceptres are in children's hands;
But more when envy breeds unkind division;
There comes the rain, there begins confusion.

Exit

SCENE II. Before Bourdeaux.

Enter TALBOT, with trump and drum

TALBOT

Go to the gates of Bourdeaux, trumpeter:
Summon their general unto the wall.

Trumpet sounds. Enter General and others, aloft

English John Talbot, captains, calls you forth,
Servant in arms to Harry King of England;
And thus he would: Open your city gates;
Be humble to us; call my sovereign yours,
And do him homage as obedient subjects;
And I'll withdraw me and my bloody power:
But, if you frown upon this proffer'd peace,
You tempt the fury of my three attendants,
Lean famine, quartering steel, and climbing fire;
Who in a moment even with the earth
Shall lay your stately and air-braving towers,
If you forsake the offer of their love.

General

Thou ominous and fearful owl of death,
Our nation's terror and their bloody scourge!
The period of thy tyranny approacheth.
On us thou canst not enter but by death;
For, I protest, we are well fortified
And strong enough to issue out and fight:
If thou retire, the Dauphin, well appointed,
Stands with the snares of war to tangle thee:
On either hand thee there are squadrons pitch'd,
To wall thee from the liberty of flight;
And no way canst thou turn thee for redress,
But death doth front thee with apparent spoil
And pale destruction meets thee in the face.
Ten thousand French have ta'en the sacrament
To rive their dangerous artillery
Upon no Christian soul but English Talbot.

Lo, there thou stand'st, a breathing valiant man,
Of an invincible unconquer'd spirit!
This is the latest glory of thy praise
That I, thy enemy, due thee withal;
For ere the glass, that now begins to run,
Finish the process of his sandy hour,
These eyes, that see thee now well coloured,
Shall see thee wither'd, bloody, pale and dead.

Drum afar off

Hark! hark! the Dauphin's drum, a warning bell,
Sings heavy music to thy timorous soul;
And mine shall ring thy dire departure out.

Exeunt General, & c

TALBOT

He fables not; I hear the enemy:
Out, some light horsemen, and peruse their wings.
O, negligent and heedless discipline!
How are we park'd and bounded in a pale,
A little herd of England's timorous deer,
Mazed with a yelping kennel of French curs!
If we be English deer, be then in blood;
Not rascal-like, to fall down with a pinch,
But rather, moody-mad and desperate stags,
Turn on the bloody hounds with heads of steel
And make the cowards stand aloof at bay:
Sell every man his life as dear as mine,
And they shall find dear deer of us, my friends.
God and Saint George, Talbot and England's right,
Prosper our colours in this dangerous fight!

Exeunt

SCENE III. Plains in Gascony.

Enter a Messenger that meets YORK. Enter YORK with trumpet and many Soldiers

YORK

Are not the speedy scouts return'd again,
That dogg'd the mighty army of the Dauphin?

Messenger

They are return'd, my lord, and give it out
That he is march'd to Bourdeaux with his power,
To fight with Talbot: as he march'd along,
By your espials were discovered
Two mightier troops than that the Dauphin led,
Which join'd with him and made their march for Bourdeaux.

YORK

A plague upon that villain Somerset,
That thus delays my promised supply
Of horsemen, that were levied for this siege!
Renowned Talbot doth expect my aid,
And I am lowted by a traitor villain
And cannot help the noble chevalier:
God comfort him in this necessity!
If he miscarry, farewell wars in France.

Enter Sir William LUCY

LUCY

Thou princely leader of our English strength,
Never so needful on the earth of France,
Spur to the rescue of the noble Talbot,
Who now is girdled with a waist of iron
And hemm'd about with grim destruction:
To Bourdeaux, warlike duke! to Bourdeaux, York!
Else, farewell Talbot, France, and England's honour.

YORK

O God, that Somerset, who in proud heart
Doth stop my cornets, were in Talbot's place!

So should we save a valiant gentleman
By forfeiting a traitor and a coward.
Mad ire and wrathful fury makes me weep,
That thus we die, while remiss traitors sleep.

LUCY

O, send some succor to the distress'd lord!

YORK

He dies, we lose; I break my warlike word;
We mourn, France smiles; we lose, they daily get;
All 'long of this vile traitor Somerset.

LUCY

Then God take mercy on brave Talbot's soul;
And on his son young John, who two hours since
I met in travel toward his warlike father!
This seven years did not Talbot see his son;
And now they meet where both their lives are done.

YORK

Alas, what joy shall noble Talbot have
To bid his young son welcome to his grave?
Away! vexation almost stops my breath,
That sunder'd friends greet in the hour of death.
Lucy, farewell; no more my fortune can,
But curse the cause I cannot aid the man.
Maine, Blois, Poictiers, and Tours, are won away,
'Long all of Somerset and his delay.

Exit, with his soldiers

LUCY

Thus, while the vulture of sedition
Feeds in the bosom of such great commanders,
Sleeping neglection doth betray to loss
The conquest of our scarce cold conqueror,
That ever living man of memory,
Henry the Fifth: whiles they each other cross,
Lives, honours, lands and all hurry to loss.

Exit

SCENE IV. Other plains in Gascony.

Enter SOMERSET, with his army; a Captain of TALBOT's with him

SOMERSET

It is too late; I cannot send them now:
This expedition was by York and Talbot
Too rashly plotted: all our general force
Might with a sally of the very town
Be buckled with: the over-daring Talbot
Hath sullied all his gloss of former honour
By this unheedful, desperate, wild adventure:
York set him on to fight and die in shame,
That, Talbot dead, great York might bear the name.

Captain

Here is Sir William Lucy, who with me
Set from our o'ermatch'd forces forth for aid.

Enter Sir William LUCY

SOMERSET

How now, Sir William! whither were you sent?

LUCY

Whither, my lord? from bought and sold Lord Talbot;
Who, ring'd about with bold adversity,
Cries out for noble York and Somerset,
To beat assailing death from his weak legions:
And whiles the honourable captain there
Drops bloody sweat from his war-wearied limbs,
And, in advantage lingering, looks for rescue,
You, his false hopes, the trust of England's honour,
Keep off aloof with worthless emulation.
Let not your private discord keep away
The levied succors that should lend him aid,
While he, renowned noble gentleman,
Yields up his life unto a world of odds:
Orleans the Bastard, Charles, Burgundy,
Alencon, Reignier, compass him about,
And Talbot perisheth by your default.

SOMERSET

York set him on; York should have sent him aid.

LUCY

And York as fast upon your grace exclaims;
Swearing that you withhold his levied host,
Collected for this expedition.

SOMERSET

York lies; he might have sent and had the horse;
I owe him little duty, and less love;
And take foul scorn to fawn on him by sending.

LUCY

The fraud of England, not the force of France,
Hath now entrapp'd the noble-minded Talbot:
Never to England shall he bear his life;
But dies, betray'd to fortune by your strife.

SOMERSET

Come, go; I will dispatch the horsemen straight:
Within six hours they will be at his aid.

LUCY

Too late comes rescue: he is ta'en or slain;
For fly he could not, if he would have fled;
And fly would Talbot never, though he might.

SOMERSET

If he be dead, brave Talbot, then adieu!

LUCY

His fame lives in the world, his shame in you.

Exeunt

SCENE V. The English camp near Bourdeaux.

Enter TALBOT and JOHN his son

TALBOT

O young John Talbot! I did send for thee
To tutor thee in stratagems of war,

That Talbot's name might be in thee revived
When sapless age and weak unable limbs
Should bring thy father to his drooping chair.
But, O malignant and ill-boding stars!
Now thou art come unto a feast of death,
A terrible and unavoided danger:
Therefore, dear boy, mount on my swiftest horse;
And I'll direct thee how thou shalt escape
By sudden flight: come, dally not, be gone.

JOHN TALBOT

Is my name Talbot? and am I your son?
And shall I fly? O if you love my mother,
Dishonour not her honourable name,
To make a bastard and a slave of me!
The world will say, he is not Talbot's blood,
That basely fled when noble Talbot stood.

TALBOT

Fly, to revenge my death, if I be slain.

JOHN TALBOT

He that flies so will ne'er return again.

TALBOT

If we both stay, we both are sure to die.

JOHN TALBOT

Then let me stay; and, father, do you fly:
Your loss is great, so your regard should be;
My worth unknown, no loss is known in me.
Upon my death the French can little boast;
In yours they will, in you all hopes are lost.
Flight cannot stain the honour you have won;
But mine it will, that no exploit have done:
You fled for vantage, everyone will swear;
But, if I bow, they'll say it was for fear.
There is no hope that ever I will stay,
If the first hour I shrink and run away.

Here on my knee I beg mortality,
Rather than life preserved with infamy.

TALBOT

Shall all thy mother's hopes lie in one tomb?

JOHN TALBOT

Ay, rather than I'll shame my mother's womb.

TALBOT

Upon my blessing, I command thee go.

JOHN TALBOT

To fight I will, but not to fly the foe.

TALBOT

Part of thy father may be saved in thee.

JOHN TALBOT

No part of him but will be shame in me.

TALBOT

Thou never hadst renown, nor canst not lose it.

JOHN TALBOT

Yes, your renowned name: shall flight abuse it?

TALBOT

Thy father's charge shall clear thee from that stain.

JOHN TALBOT

You cannot witness for me, being slain.
If death be so apparent, then both fly.

TALBOT

And leave my followers here to fight and die?
My age was never tainted with such shame.

JOHN TALBOT

And shall my youth be guilty of such blame?
No more can I be sever'd from your side,
Than can yourself yourself in twain divide:

Stay, go, do what you will, the like do I;
For live I will not, if my father die.

TALBOT

Then here I take my leave of thee, fair son,
Born to eclipse thy life this afternoon.
Come, side by side together live and die.
And soul with soul from France to heaven fly.

Exeunt

SCENE VI. A field of battle.

*Alarum: excursions, wherein JOHN TALBOT is hemmed about, and
TALBOT rescues him*

TALBOT

Saint George and victory! fight, soldiers, fight.
The regent hath with Talbot broke his word
And left us to the rage of France his sword.
Where is John Talbot? Pause, and take thy breath;
I gave thee life and rescued thee from death.

JOHN TALBOT

O, twice my father, twice am I thy son!
The life thou gavest me first was lost and done,
Till with thy warlike sword, despite of late,
To my determined time thou gavest new date.

TALBOT

When from the Dauphin's crest thy sword struck fire,
It warm'd thy father's heart with proud desire
Of bold-faced victory. Then leaden age,
Quicken'd with youthful spleen and warlike rage,
Beat down Alencon, Orleans, Burgundy,
And from the pride of Gallia rescued thee.
The ireful bastard Orleans, that drew blood
From thee, my boy, and had the maidenhood
Of thy first fight, I soon encountered,
And interchanging blows I quickly shed

Some of his bastard blood; and in disgrace
Bespoke him thus; 'Contaminated, base
And misbegotten blood I spill of thine,
Mean and right poor, for that pure blood of mine
Which thou didst force from Talbot, my brave boy:'
Here, purposing the Bastard to destroy,
Came in strong rescue. Speak, thy father's care,
Art thou not weary, John? how dost thou fare?
Wilt thou yet leave the battle, boy, and fly,
Now thou art seal'd the son of chivalry?
Fly, to revenge my death when I am dead:
The help of one stands me in little stead.
O, too much folly is it, well I wot,
To hazard all our lives in one small boat!
If I to-day die not with Frenchmen's rage,
To-morrow I shall die with mickle age:
By me they nothing gain an if I stay;
'Tis but the shortening of my life one day:
In thee thy mother dies, our household's name,
My death's revenge, thy youth, and England's fame:
All these and more we hazard by thy stay;
All these are saved if thou wilt fly away.

JOHN TALBOT

The sword of Orleans hath not made me smart;
These words of yours draw life-blood from my heart:
On that advantage, bought with such a shame,
To save a paltry life and slay bright fame,
Before young Talbot from old Talbot fly,
The coward horse that bears me fail and die!
And like me to the peasant boys of France,
To be shame's scorn and subject of mischance!
Surely, by all the glory you have won,
An if I fly, I am not Talbot's son:
Then talk no more of flight, it is no boot;
If son to Talbot, die at Talbot's foot.

TALBOT

Then follow thou thy desperate sire of Crete,
Thou Icarus; thy life to me is sweet:
If thou wilt fight, fight by thy father's side;
And, commendable proved, let's die in pride.

Exeunt

SCENE VII. Another part of the field.

Alarum: excursions. Enter TALBOT led by a Servant

TALBOT

Where is my other life? mine own is gone;
O, where's young Talbot? where is valiant John?
Triumphant death, smear'd with captivity,
Young Talbot's valour makes me smile at thee:
When he perceived me shrink and on my knee,
His bloody sword he brandish'd over me,
And, like a hungry lion, did commence
Rough deeds of rage and stern impatience;
But when my angry guardant stood alone,
Tendering my ruin and assail'd of none,
Dizzy-eyed fury and great rage of heart
Suddenly made him from my side to start
Into the clustering battle of the French;
And in that sea of blood my boy did drench
His over-mounting spirit, and there died,
My Icarus, my blossom, in his pride.

Servant

O, my dear lord, lo, where your son is borne!

Enter Soldiers, with the body of JOHN TALBOT

TALBOT

Thou antic death, which laugh'st us here to scorn,
Anon, from thy insulting tyranny,
Coupled in bonds of perpetuity,
Two Talbots, winged through the lither sky,

In thy despite shall 'scape mortality.
O, thou, whose wounds become hard-favour'd death,
Speak to thy father ere thou yield thy breath!
Brave death by speaking, whether he will or no;
Imagine him a Frenchman and thy foe.
Poor boy! he smiles, methinks, as who should say,
Had death been French, then death had died to-day.
Come, come and lay him in his father's arms:
My spirit can no longer bear these harms.
Soldiers, adieu! I have what I would have,
Now my old arms are young John Talbot's grave.

Dies

Enter CHARLES, ALENCON, BURGUNDY, BASTARD OF ORLEANS,
JOAN LA PUCELLE, and forces

CHARLES

Had York and Somerset brought rescue in,
We should have found a bloody day of this.

BASTARD OF ORLEANS

How the young whelp of Talbot's, raging-wood,
Did flesh his puny sword in Frenchmen's blood!

JOAN LA PUCELLE

Once I encounter'd him, and thus I said:
'Thou maiden youth, be vanquish'd by a maid:'
But, with a proud majestical high scorn,
He answer'd thus: 'Young Talbot was not born
To be the pillage of a giglot wench:'
So, rushing in the bowels of the French,
He left me proudly, as unworthy fight.

BURGUNDY

Doubtless he would have made a noble knight;
See, where he lies inhearsed in the arms
Of the most bloody nurser of his harms!

BASTARD OF ORLEANS

Hew them to pieces, hack their bones asunder
Whose life was England's glory, Gallia's wonder.

CHARLES

O, no, forbear! for that which we have fled
During the life, let us not wrong it dead.

Enter Sir William LUCY, attended; Herald of the French preceding

LUCY

Herald, conduct me to the Dauphin's tent,
To know who hath obtained the glory of the day.

CHARLES

On what submissive message art thou sent?

LUCY

Submission, Dauphin! 'tis a mere French word;
We English warriors wot not what it means.
I come to know what prisoners thou hast ta'en
And to survey the bodies of the dead.

CHARLES

For prisoners ask'st thou? hell our prison is.
But tell me whom thou seek'st.

LUCY

But where's the great Alcides of the field,
Valiant Lord Talbot, Earl of Shrewsbury,
Created, for his rare success in arms,
Great Earl of Washford, Waterford and Valence;
Lord Talbot of Goodrig and Urchinfield,
Lord Strange of Blackmere, Lord Verdun of Alton,
Lord Cromwell of Wingfield, Lord Furnival of Sheffield,
The thrice-victorious Lord of Falconbridge;
Knight of the noble order of Saint George,
Worthy Saint Michael and the Golden Fleece;
Great marshal to Henry the Sixth
Of all his wars within the realm of France?

JOAN LA PUCELLE

Here is a silly stately style indeed!
The Turk, that two and fifty kingdoms hath,

Writes not so tedious a style as this.
Him that thou magnifiest with all these titles
Stinking and fly-blown lies here at our feet.

LUCY

Is Talbot slain, the Frenchmen's only scourge,
Your kingdom's terror and black Nemesis?
O, were mine eyeballs into bullets turn'd,
That I in rage might shoot them at your faces!
O, that I could but call these dead to life!
It were enough to fright the realm of France:
Were but his picture left amongst you here,
It would amaze the proudest of you all.
Give me their bodies, that I may bear them hence
And give them burial as beseems their worth.

JOAN LA PUCELLE

I think this upstart is old Talbot's ghost,
He speaks with such a proud commanding spirit.
For God's sake let him have 'em; to keep them here,
They would but stink, and putrefy the air.

CHARLES

Go, take their bodies hence.

LUCY

I'll bear them hence; but from their ashes shall be rear'd
A phoenix that shall make all France afeard.

CHARLES

So we be rid of them, do with 'em what thou wilt.
And now to Paris, in this conquering vein:
All will be ours, now bloody Talbot's slain.

Exeunt

ACT V

SCENE I. London. The palace.

Sennet. Enter KING HENRY VI, GLOUCESTER, and EXETER

KING HENRY VI

Have you perused the letters from the pope,
The emperor and the Earl of Armagnac?

GLOUCESTER

I have, my lord: and their intent is this:
They humbly sue unto your excellence
To have a godly peace concluded of
Between the realms of England and of France.

KING HENRY VI

How doth your grace affect their motion?

GLOUCESTER

Well, my good lord; and as the only means
To stop effusion of our Christian blood
And 'stablish quietness on every side.

KING HENRY VI

Ay, marry, uncle; for I always thought
It was both impious and unnatural
That such immanity and bloody strife
Should reign among professors of one faith.

GLOUCESTER

Beside, my lord, the sooner to effect
And surer bind this knot of amity,

The Earl of Armagnac, near knit to Charles,
A man of great authority in France,
Proffers his only daughter to your grace
In marriage, with a large and sumptuous dowry.

KING HENRY VI

Marriage, uncle! alas, my years are young!
And fitter is my study and my books
Than wanton dalliance with a paramour.
Yet call the ambassador; and, as you please,
So let them have their answers every one:
I shall be well content with any choice
Tends to God's glory and my country's weal.

Enter CARDINAL OF WINCHESTER in Cardinal's habit, a Legate and two Ambassadors

EXETER

What! is my Lord of Winchester install'd,
And call'd unto a cardinal's degree?
Then I perceive that will be verified
Henry the Fifth did sometime prophesy,
'If once he come to be a cardinal,
He'll make his cap co-equal with the crown.'

KING HENRY VI

My lords ambassadors, your several suits
Have been consider'd and debated on.
And therefore are we certainly resolved
To draw conditions of a friendly peace;
Which by my Lord of Winchester we mean
Shall be transported presently to France.

GLOUCESTER

And for the proffer of my lord your master,
I have inform'd his highness so at large
As liking of the lady's virtuous gifts,
Her beauty and the value of her dower,
He doth intend she shall be England's queen.

KING HENRY VI

In argument and proof of which contract,
Bear her this jewel, pledge of my affection.
And so, my lord protector, see them guarded
And safely brought to Dover; where inshipp'd
Commit them to the fortune of the sea.

Exeunt all but CARDINAL OF WINCHESTER and Legate

CARDINAL

OF WINCHESTER

Stay, my lord legate: you shall first receive
The sum of money which I promised
Should be deliver'd to his holiness
For clothing me in these grave ornaments.

Legate

I will attend upon your lordship's leisure.
CARDINAL

OF WINCHESTER

[Aside] Now Winchester will not submit, I trow,
Or be inferior to the proudest peer.
Humphrey of Gloucester, thou shalt well perceive
That, neither in birth or for authority,
The bishop will be overborne by thee:
I'll either make thee stoop and bend thy knee,
Or sack this country with a mutiny.

Exeunt

SCENE II. France. Plains in Anjou.

*Enter CHARLES, BURGUNDY, ALENCON, BASTARD OF ORLEANS,
REIGNIER, JOAN LA PUCELLE, and forces*

CHARLES

These news, my lord, may cheer our drooping spirits:
'Tis said the stout Parisians do revolt
And turn again unto the warlike French.

ALENCON

Then march to Paris, royal Charles of France,
And keep not back your powers in dalliance.

JOAN LA PUCELLE

Peace be amongst them, if they turn to us;
Else, ruin combat with their palaces!

Enter Scout

Scout

Success unto our valiant general,
And happiness to his accomplices!

CHARLES

What tidings send our scouts? I prithee, speak.

Scout

The English army, that divided was
Into two parties, is now conjoined in one,
And means to give you battle presently.

CHARLES

Somewhat too sudden, sirs, the warning is;
But we will presently provide for them.

BURGUNDY

I trust the ghost of Talbot is not there:
Now he is gone, my lord, you need not fear.

JOAN LA PUCELLE

Of all base passions, fear is most accursed.
Command the conquest, Charles, it shall be thine,
Let Henry fret and all the world repine.

CHARLES

Then on, my lords; and France be fortunate!

Exeunt

SCENE III. Before Angiers.

Alarum. Excursions. Enter JOAN LA PUCELLE

JOAN LA PUCELLE

The regent conquers, and the Frenchmen fly.
Now help, ye charming spells and periapts;
And ye choice spirits that admonish me
And give me signs of future accidents.

Thunder

You speedy helpers, that are substitutes
Under the lordly monarch of the north,
Appear and aid me in this enterprise.

Enter Fiends

This speedy and quick appearance argues proof
Of your accustom'd diligence to me.
Now, ye familiar spirits, that are cull'd
Out of the powerful regions under earth,
Help me this once, that France may get the field.

They walk, and speak not

O, hold me not with silence over-long!
Where I was wont to feed you with my blood,
I'll lop a member off and give it you
In earnest of further benefit,
So you do condescend to help me now.

They hang their heads

No hope to have redress? My body shall
Pay recompense, if you will grant my suit.

They shake their heads

Cannot my body nor blood-sacrifice
Entreat you to your wonted furtherance?
Then take my soul, my body, soul and all,
Before that England give the French the foil.

They depart

See, they forsake me! Now the time is come
That France must vail her lofty-plumed crest

And let her head fall into England's lap.
My ancient incantations are too weak,
And hell too strong for me to buckle with:
Now, France, thy glory droopeth to the dust.

Exit

Excursions. Re-enter JOAN LA PUCELLE fighting hand to hand with
YORK. JOAN LA PUCELLE is taken. The French fly.

YORK

Damsel of France, I think I have you fast:
Unchain your spirits now with spelling charms
And try if they can gain your liberty.
A goodly prize, fit for the devil's grace!
See, how the ugly wench doth bend her brows,
As if with Circe she would change my shape!

JOAN LA PUCELLE

Changed to a worser shape thou canst not be.

YORK

O, Charles the Dauphin is a proper man;
No shape but his can please your dainty eye.

JOAN LA PUCELLE

A plaguing mischief light on Charles and thee!
And may ye both be suddenly surprised
By bloody hands, in sleeping on your beds!

YORK

Fell banning hag, enchantress, hold thy tongue!

JOAN LA PUCELLE

I prithee, give me leave to curse awhile.

YORK

Curse, miscreant, when thou comest to the stake.

Exeunt

Alarum. Enter SUFFOLK with MARGARET in his hand

SUFFOLK

Be what thou wilt, thou art my prisoner.

Gazes on her
O fairest beauty, do not fear nor fly!
For I will touch thee but with reverent hands;
I kiss these fingers for eternal peace,
And lay them gently on thy tender side.
Who art thou? say, that I may honour thee.

MARGARET

Margaret my name, and daughter to a king,
The King of Naples, whosoe'er thou art.

SUFFOLK

An earl I am, and Suffolk am I call'd.
Be not offended, nature's miracle,
Thou art allotted to be ta'en by me:
So doth the swan her downy cygnets save,
Keeping them prisoner underneath her wings.
Yet, if this servile usage once offend.
Go, and be free again, as Suffolk's friend.

She is going
O, stay! I have no power to let her pass;
My hand would free her, but my heart says no
As plays the sun upon the glassy streams,
Twinkling another counterfeited beam,
So seems this gorgeous beauty to mine eyes.
Fain would I woo her, yet I dare not speak:
I'll call for pen and ink, and write my mind.
Fie, de la Pole! disable not thyself;
Hast not a tongue? is she not here?
Wilt thou be daunted at a woman's sight?
Ay, beauty's princely majesty is such,
Confounds the tongue and makes the senses rough.

MARGARET

Say, Earl of Suffolk--if thy name be so--
What ransom must I pay before I pass?
For I perceive I am thy prisoner.

SUFFOLK

How canst thou tell she will deny thy suit,
Before thou make a trial of her love?

MARGARET

Why speak'st thou not? what ransom must I pay?

SUFFOLK

She's beautiful, and therefore to be woo'd;
She is a woman, therefore to be won.

MARGARET

Wilt thou accept of ransom? yea, or no.

SUFFOLK

Fond man, remember that thou hast a wife;
Then how can Margaret be thy paramour?

MARGARET

I were best to leave him, for he will not hear.

SUFFOLK

There all is marr'd; there lies a cooling card.

MARGARET

He talks at random; sure, the man is mad.

SUFFOLK

And yet a dispensation may be had.

MARGARET

And yet I would that you would answer me.

SUFFOLK

I'll win this Lady Margaret. For whom?
Why, for my king: tush, that's a wooden thing!

MARGARET

He talks of wood: it is some carpenter.

SUFFOLK

Yet so my fancy may be satisfied,
And peace established between these realms

But there remains a scruple in that too;
For though her father be the King of Naples,
Duke of Anjou and Maine, yet is he poor,
And our nobility will scorn the match.

MARGARET

Hear ye, captain, are you not at leisure?

SUFFOLK

It shall be so, disdain they ne'er so much.
Henry is youthful and will quickly yield.
Madam, I have a secret to reveal.

MARGARET

What though I be enthrall'd? he seems a knight,
And will not any way dishonour me.

SUFFOLK

Lady, vouchsafe to listen what I say.

MARGARET

Perhaps I shall be rescued by the French;
And then I need not crave his courtesy.

SUFFOLK

Sweet madam, give me a hearing in a cause--

MARGARET

Tush, women have been captivate ere now.

SUFFOLK

Lady, wherefore talk you so?

MARGARET

I cry you mercy, 'tis but Quid for Quo.

SUFFOLK

Say, gentle princess, would you not suppose
Your bondage happy, to be made a queen?

MARGARET

To be a queen in bondage is more vile
Than is a slave in base servility;
For princes should be free.

SUFFOLK

And so shall you,
If happy England's royal king be free.

MARGARET

Why, what concerns his freedom unto me?

SUFFOLK

I'll undertake to make thee Henry's queen,
To put a golden sceptre in thy hand
And set a precious crown upon thy head,
If thou wilt condescend to be my--

MARGARET

What?

SUFFOLK

His love.

MARGARET

I am unworthy to be Henry's wife.

SUFFOLK

No, gentle madam; I unworthy am
To woo so fair a dame to be his wife,
And have no portion in the choice myself.
How say you, madam, are ye so content?

MARGARET

An if my father please, I am content.

SUFFOLK

Then call our captains and our colours forth.
And, madam, at your father's castle walls
We'll crave a parley, to confer with him.

A parley sounded. Enter REIGNIER on the walls

See, Reignier, see, thy daughter prisoner!

REIGNIER

To whom?

SUFFOLK

To me.

REIGNIER

Suffolk, what remedy?
I am a soldier, and unapt to weep,
Or to exclaim on fortune's fickleness.

SU FFOLK

Yes, there is remedy enough, my lord:
Consent, and for thy honour give consent,
Thy daughter shall be wedded to my king;
Whom I with pain have woo'd and won thereto;
And this her easy-held imprisonment
Hath gained thy daughter princely liberty.

REIGNIER

Speaks Suffolk as he thinks?

SUFFOLK

Fair Margaret knows
That Suffolk doth not flatter, face, or feign.

REIGNIER

Upon thy princely warrant, I descend
To give thee answer of thy just demand.

Exit from the walls

SUFFOLK

And here I will expect thy coming.

Trumpets sound. Enter REIGNIER, below

REIGNIER

Welcome, brave earl, into our territories:
Command in Anjou what your honour pleases.

SUFFOLK

Thanks, Reignier, happy for so sweet a child,
Fit to be made companion with a king:
What answer makes your grace unto my suit?

REIGNIER

Since thou dost deign to woo her little worth
To be the princely bride of such a lord;
Upon condition I may quietly
Enjoy mine own, the country Maine and Anjou,
Free from oppression or the stroke of war,
My daughter shall be Henry's, if he please.

SUFFOLK

That is her ransom; I deliver her;
And those two counties I will undertake
Your grace shall well and quietly enjoy.

REIGNIER

And I again, in Henry's royal name,
As deputy unto that gracious king,
Give thee her hand, for sign of plighted faith.

SUFFOLK

Reignier of France, I give thee kingly thanks,
Because this is in traffic of a king.

Aside

And yet, methinks, I could be well content
To be mine own attorney in this case.
I'll over then to England with this news,
And make this marriage to be solemnized.
So farewell, Reignier: set this diamond safe
In golden palaces, as it becomes.

REIGNIER

I do embrace thee, as I would embrace
The Christian prince, King Henry, were he here.

MARGARET

Farewell, my lord: good wishes, praise and prayers
Shall Suffolk ever have of Margaret.

Going

SUFFOLK

Farewell, sweet madam: but hark you, Margaret;
No princely commendations to my king?

MARGARET

Such commendations as becomes a maid,
A virgin and his servant, say to him.

SUFFOLK

Words sweetly placed and modestly directed.
But madam, I must trouble you again;
No loving token to his majesty?

MARGARET

Yes, my good lord, a pure unspotted heart,
Never yet taint with love, I send the king.

SUFFOLK

And this withal.

Kisses her

MARGARET

That for thyself: I will not so presume
To send such peevish tokens to a king.

Exeunt REIGNIER and MARGARET

SUFFOLK

O, wert thou for myself! But, Suffolk, stay;
Thou mayst not wander in that labyrinth;
There Minotaurs and ugly treasons lurk.
Solicit Henry with her wondrous praise:
Bethink thee on her virtues that surmount,
And natural graces that extinguish art;
Repeat their semblance often on the seas,

That, when thou comest to kneel at Henry's feet,
Thou mayst bereave him of his wits with wonder.

Exit

SCENE IV. Camp of the YORK in Anjou.

Enter YORK, WARWICK, and others

YORK

Bring forth that sorceress condemn'd to burn.

Enter JOAN LA PUCELLE, guarded, and a Shepherd

Shepherd

Ah, Joan, this kills thy father's heart outright!
Have I sought every country far and near,
And, now it is my chance to find thee out,
Must I behold thy timeless cruel death?
Ah, Joan, sweet daughter Joan, I'll die with thee!

JOAN LA PUCELLE

Decrepit miser! base ignoble wretch!
I am descended of a gentler blood:
Thou art no father nor no friend of mine.

Shepherd

Out, out! My lords, an please you, 'tis not so;
I did beget her, all the parish knows:
Her mother liveth yet, can testify
She was the first fruit of my bachelorship.

WARWICK

Graceless! wilt thou deny thy parentage?

YORK

This argues what her kind of life hath been,
Wicked and vile; and so her death concludes.

Shepherd

Fie, Joan, that thou wilt be so obstacle!
God knows thou art a collop of my flesh;

And for thy sake have I shed many a tear:
Deny me not, I prithee, gentle Joan.

JOAN LA PUCELLE

Peasant, avaunt! You have suborn'd this man,
Of purpose to obscure my noble birth.

Shepherd

'Tis true, I gave a noble to the priest
The morn that I was wedded to her mother.
Kneel down and take my blessing, good my girl.
Wilt thou not stoop? Now cursed be the time
Of thy nativity! I would the milk
Thy mother gave thee when thou suck'dst her breast,
Had been a little ratsbane for thy sake!
Or else, when thou didst keep my lambs a-field,
I wish some ravenous wolf had eaten thee!
Dost thou deny thy father, cursed drab?
O, burn her, burn her! hanging is too good.

Exit

YORK

Take her away; for she hath lived too long,
To fill the world with vicious qualities.

JOAN LA PUCELLE

First, let me tell you whom you have condemn'd:
Not me begotten of a shepherd swain,
But issued from the progeny of kings;
Virtuous and holy; chosen from above,
By inspiration of celestial grace,
To work exceeding miracles on earth.
I never had to do with wicked spirits:
But you, that are polluted with your lusts,
Stain'd with the guiltless blood of innocents,
Corrupt and tainted with a thousand vices,
Because you want the grace that others have,
You judge it straight a thing impossible
To compass wonders but by help of devils.

No, misconceived! Joan of Arc hath been
A virgin from her tender infancy,
Chaste and immaculate in very thought;
Whose maiden blood, thus rigorously effused,
Will cry for vengeance at the gates of heaven.

YORK

Ay, ay: away with her to execution!

WARWICK

And hark ye, sirs; because she is a maid,
Spare for no faggots, let there be enow:
Place barrels of pitch upon the fatal stake,
That so her torture may be shortened.

JOAN LA PUCELLE

Will nothing turn your unrelenting hearts?
Then, Joan, discover thine infirmity,
That warranteth by law to be thy privilege.
I am with child, ye bloody homicides:
Murder not then the fruit within my womb,
Although ye hale me to a violent death.

YORK

Now heaven forfend! the holy maid with child!

WARWICK

The greatest miracle that e'er ye wrought:
Is all your strict preciseness come to this?

YORK

She and the Dauphin have been juggling:
I did imagine what would be her refuge.

WARWICK

Well, go to; we'll have no bastards live;
Especially since Charles must father it.

JOAN LA PUCELLE

You are deceived; my child is none of his:
It was Alencon that enjoy'd my love.

YORK

Alencon! that notorious Machiavel!
It dies, an if it had a thousand lives.

JOAN LA PUCELLE

O, give me leave, I have deluded you:
'Twas neither Charles nor yet the duke I named,
But Reignier, king of Naples, that prevail'd.

WARWICK

A married man! that's most intolerable.

YORK

Why, here's a girl! I think she knows not well,
There were so many, whom she may accuse.

WARWICK

It's sign she hath been liberal and free.

YORK

And yet, forsooth, she is a virgin pure.
Strumpet, thy words condemn thy brat and thee:
Use no entreaty, for it is in vain.

JOAN LA PUCELLE

Then lead me hence; with whom I leave my curse:
May never glorious sun reflex his beams
Upon the country where you make abode;
But darkness and the gloomy shade of death
Environ you, till mischief and despair
Drive you to break your necks or hang yourselves!

Exit, guarded

YORK

Break thou in pieces and consume to ashes,
Thou foul accursed minister of hell!

Enter CARDINAL OF WINCHESTER, attended

CARDINAL

OF WINCHESTER

Lord regent, I do greet your excellence
With letters of commission from the king.
For know, my lords, the states of Christendom,
Moved with remorse of these outrageous broils,
Have earnestly implored a general peace
Betwixt our nation and the aspiring French;
And here at hand the Dauphin and his train
Approacheth, to confer about some matter.

YORK

Is all our travail turn'd to this effect?
After the slaughter of so many peers,
So many captains, gentlemen and soldiers,
That in this quarrel have been overthrown
And sold their bodies for their country's benefit,
Shall we at last conclude effeminate peace?
Have we not lost most part of all the towns,
By treason, falsehood and by treachery,
Our great progenitors had conquered?
O Warwick, Warwick! I foresee with grief
The utter loss of all the realm of France.

WARWICK

Be patient, York: if we conclude a peace,
It shall be with such strict and severe covenants
As little shall the Frenchmen gain thereby.

Enter CHARLES, ALENCON, BASTARD OF ORLEANS, REIGNIER, and others

CHARLES

Since, lords of England, it is thus agreed
That peaceful truce shall be proclaim'd in France,
We come to be informed by yourselves
What the conditions of that league must be.

YORK

Speak, Winchester; for boiling choler chokes
The hollow passage of my poison'd voice,

By sight of these our baleful enemies.

CARDINAL

OF WINCHESTER

Charles, and the rest, it is enacted thus:
That, in regard King Henry gives consent,
Of mere compassion and of lenity,
To ease your country of distressful war,
And suffer you to breathe in fruitful peace,
You shall become true liegemen to his crown:
And Charles, upon condition thou wilt swear
To pay him tribute, submit thyself,
Thou shalt be placed as viceroy under him,
And still enjoy thy regal dignity.

ALENCON

Must he be then as shadow of himself?
Adorn his temples with a coronet,
And yet, in substance and authority,
Retain but privilege of a private man?
This proffer is absurd and reasonless.

CHARLES

'Tis known already that I am possess'd
With more than half the Gallian territories,
And therein reverenced for their lawful king:
Shall I, for lucre of the rest unvanquish'd,
Detract so much from that prerogative,
As to be call'd but viceroy of the whole?
No, lord ambassador, I'll rather keep
That which I have than, coveting for more,
Be cast from possibility of all.

YORK

Insulting Charles! hast thou by secret means
Used intercession to obtain a league,
And, now the matter grows to compromise,
Stand'st thou aloof upon comparison?
Either accept the title thou usurp'st,

Of benefit proceeding from our king
And not of any challenge of desert,
Or we will plague thee with incessant wars.

REIGNIER

My lord, you do not well in obstinacy
To cavil in the course of this contract:
If once it be neglected, ten to one
We shall not find like opportunity.

ALENCON

To say the truth, it is your policy
To save your subjects from such massacre
And ruthless slaughters as are daily seen
By our proceeding in hostility;
And therefore take this compact of a truce,
Although you break it when your pleasure serves.

WARWICK

How say'st thou, Charles? shall our condition stand?

CHARLES

It shall;
Only reserved, you claim no interest
In any of our towns of garrison.

YORK

Then swear allegiance to his majesty,
As thou art knight, never to disobey
Nor be rebellious to the crown of England,
Thou, nor thy nobles, to the crown of England.
So, now dismiss your army when ye please:
Hang up your ensign, let your drums be still,
For here we entertain a solemn peace.

Exeunt

SCENE V. London. The palace.

Enter SUFFOLK in conference with KING HENRY VI, GLOUCESTER and EXETER

KING HENRY VI

Your wondrous rare description, noble earl,
Of beauteous Margaret hath astonish'd me:
Her virtues graced with external gifts
Do breed love's settled passions in my heart:
And like as rigor of tempestuous gusts
Provokes the mightiest hulk against the tide,
So am I driven by breath of her renown
Either to suffer shipwreck or arrive
Where I may have fruition of her love.

SUFFOLK

Tush, my good lord, this superficial tale
Is but a preface of her worthy praise;
The chief perfections of that lovely dame
Had I sufficient skill to utter them,
Would make a volume of enticing lines,
Able to ravish any dull conceit:
And, which is more, she is not so divine,
So full-replete with choice of all delights,
But with as humble lowliness of mind
She is content to be at your command;
Command, I mean, of virtuous chaste intents,
To love and honour Henry as her lord.

KING HENRY VI

And otherwise will Henry ne'er presume.
Therefore, my lord protector, give consent
That Margaret may be England's royal queen.

GLOUCESTER

So should I give consent to flatter sin.
You know, my lord, your highness is betroth'd
Unto another lady of esteem:

How shall we then dispense with that contract,
And not deface your honour with reproach?

SUFFOLK

As doth a ruler with unlawful oaths;
Or one that, at a triumph having vow'd
To try his strength, forsaketh yet the lists
By reason of his adversary's odds:
A poor earl's daughter is unequal odds,
And therefore may be broke without offence.

GLOUCESTER

Why, what, I pray, is Margaret more than that?
Her father is no better than an earl,
Although in glorious titles he excel.

SUFFOLK

Yes, lord, her father is a king,
The King of Naples and Jerusalem;
And of such great authority in France
As his alliance will confirm our peace
And keep the Frenchmen in allegiance.

GLOUCESTER

And so the Earl of Armagnac may do,
Because he is near kinsman unto Charles.

EXETER

Beside, his wealth doth warrant a liberal dower,
Where Reignier sooner will receive than give.

SUFFOLK

A dower, my lords! disgrace not so your king,
That he should be so abject, base and poor,
To choose for wealth and not for perfect love.
Henry is able to enrich his queen
And not seek a queen to make him rich:
So worthless peasants bargain for their wives,
As market-men for oxen, sheep, or horse.
Marriage is a matter of more worth

Than to be dealt in by attorneyship;
Not whom we will, but whom his grace affects,
Must be companion of his nuptial bed:
And therefore, lords, since he affects her most,
It most of all these reasons bindeth us,
In our opinions she should be preferr'd.
For what is wedlock forced but a hell,
An age of discord and continual strife?
Whereas the contrary bringeth bliss,
And is a pattern of celestial peace.
Whom should we match with Henry, being a king,
But Margaret, that is daughter to a king?
Her peerless feature, joined with her birth,
Approves her fit for none but for a king:
Her valiant courage and undaunted spirit,
More than in women commonly is seen,
Will answer our hope in issue of a king;
For Henry, son unto a conqueror,
Is likely to beget more conquerors,
If with a lady of so high resolve
As is fair Margaret he be link'd in love.
Then yield, my lords; and here conclude with me
That Margaret shall be queen, and none but she.

KING HENRY VI

Whether it be through force of your report,
My noble Lord of Suffolk, or for that
My tender youth was never yet attaint
With any passion of inflaming love,
I cannot tell; but this I am assured,
I feel such sharp dissension in my breast,
Such fierce alarums both of hope and fear,
As I am sick with working of my thoughts.
Take, therefore, shipping; post, my lord, to France;
Agree to any covenants, and procure
That Lady Margaret do vouchsafe to come
To cross the seas to England and be crown'd
King Henry's faithful and anointed queen:

For your expenses and sufficient charge,
Among the people gather up a tenth.
Be gone, I say; for, till you do return,
I rest perplexed with a thousand cares.
And you, good uncle, banish all offence:
If you do censure me by what you were,
Not what you are, I know it will excuse
This sudden execution of my will.
And so, conduct me where, from company,
I may revolve and ruminate my grief.

Exit

GLOUCESTER

Ay, grief, I fear me, both at first and last.

Exeunt GLOUCESTER and EXETER

SUFFOLK

Thus Suffolk hath prevail'd; and thus he goes,
As did the youthful Paris once to Greece,
With hope to find the like event in love,
But prosper better than the Trojan did.
Margaret shall now be queen, and rule the king;
But I will rule both her, the king and realm.

Exit

www.freeclassicebooks.com